ESCAPE.

THE COMPLETE AGORAPHOBIA RECOVERY COURSE

By Joseph O'Neill

Joseph O'Neill

Published by
Chipmunkapublishing
PO Box 6872
Brentwood
Essex CM13 1ZT
United Kingdom

http://www.chipmunkapublishing.com

Edited by Belinda Amobire

ESCAPE!

INTRODUCTION

CHAPTER 1 My Story – Your Story.

- ➤ My Story
- ➤ Your Story
- ➤ Action Points

CHAPTER 2 What is Agoraphobia?

- ➤ The need to know.
- ➤ What agoraphobia is not.
- ➤ Definition.
- ➤ Test your understanding.
- ➤ How agoraphobia starts and develops.
- ➤ Who becomes agoraphobic?
- ➤ The truth shall make you free.
- ➤ The origins of agoraphobia.
- ➤ What is happening?
- ➤ Learning to be agoraphobic.
- ➤ How we build a lifestyle around agoraphobia.
- ➤ Anxiety.
- ➤ The impact of agoraphobia on your life.
- ➤ What is really happening?
- ➤ Are you agoraphobic?
- ➤ Panic attacks.
- ➤ What is a panic attack?
- ➤ Checklist of symptoms.

➢ The development of panics.
➢ What is happening during a panic attack?

CHAPTER 3 What Therapies are Available?

➢ Available Therapies
➢ Drug Therapy
➢ Psychoanalysis
➢ Learning Therapy
➢ Hypnosis
➢ Behavioural Therapy
➢ The Benefits of Self-Help
➢ What it takes to Succeed
➢ Making a Commitment to Recovery
➢ Choose Life!
➢ Action Points

CHAPTER 4 Self Esteem

➢ Loss of confidence
➢ Getting started
➢ Telling others
➢ What we believe
➢ Strategies for restoring self-esteem
➢ Dealing with guilt
➢ Self-talk
➢ Action Point
➢ Worry
➢ Breaking the chain
➢ Shifting the focus

ESCAPE!

- ➤ Accentuate the positive
- ➤ Action Point
- ➤ Planning
- ➤ Action Point
- ➤ Coming off tranquillisers
- ➤ Goals
- ➤ Action Point
- ➤ Making Excuses

CHAPTER 5 Countering Panic

- ➤ What panic can't do
- ➤ Coping with panic: strategies to defuse fear:
- ✓ Acceptance
- ✓ Positive self-talk
- ✓ Concentrating on what is happening
- ✓ Coping statements
- ✓ Countering physical symptoms
- ✓ Alternative Nostril Breathing
- ✓ Distraction
- ✓ Emergency measures

CHAPTER 6 Meditation / Yoga / Progressive Relaxation

- ➤ Anxiety is not a permanent condition
- ➤ Meditation: the facts
- ➤ Practising meditation.
- ➤ Points to note
- ➤ Yoga
- ➤ Progressive Muscle Relaxation

ESCAPE!

APPENDIX

Photocopiable worksheets and record-keeping sheets related to strategies outlined in text.

- ➢ Self-help books
- ➢ Useful websites
- ➢ Associations offering advice and support to agoraphobics

ESCAPE!

AGORAPHOBIA

INTRODUCTION

I am an agoraphobic, writing this for other agoraphobics.

For thirty years I battled against an illness that threatened to swamp me. My self-esteem evaporated. I lost hope. The pressure on my marriage became intolerable. My career was under threat. Trapped in a downward spiral, battered by depression and anxiety, I felt doomed to exist in a shrinking world.

Yet today I am symptom-free. I travel abroad several times a year and enjoy a full life. Panic attacks are a memory.

But the ordeal of agoraphobia was not for nothing.

During those thirty years I tried the full range of therapies. Some helped. Others made my condition worse, prolonged my illness and created problems as bad as those they were intended to solve. Only one fully addressed the problem and broke down the barriers to a full life.

I know what is involved in each type of therapy. I know what worked for me
-- and I know it as only an agoraphobic can. You can benefit from my experiences, from the bad as much as the good.

The biggest mistake I made was denial. For a long time I refused to accept that I was ill. I stuck to the groundless belief that my symptoms would melt away without any effort on my part. Meantime, I told myself, all I had to do was conceal my fears and stay away from the things that frightened me.

Little did I know that what I was doing was allowing my fears to bed in and establish roots. Every time I avoided a lift, walked instead of getting the bus or made elaborate arrangements so I wasn't alone, I was nourishing my phobias, helping them to flourish until they invaded every facet of my life.

Only when I refused to accept them and their restrictions did I make any progress. This was the first step to recovery.

Do not tolerate your illness as your lot in life. No matter how bad you feel today, you can get better. Agoraphobia is a life sentence only if you accept it. No matter how long you have suffered, no matter what you have told yourself in the past, agoraphobia is a curable condition. There is only one obstacle to your full recovery.

ESCAPE!

Without determination you will not succeed. You may have the best therapy in the world, the most supportive family and friends, a clear understanding of your illness and how to overcome it, but without grit you will achieve nothing.

There is no quick fix, no panacea, no tablet that will dissolve your fears. Recovery is a long haul on a bumpy road. You will have setbacks and disappointments. There will be times when you feel you are making no progress and are even going backwards. Some days you'll seethe with anger and frustration. On occasion you'll feel worn down by the challenges of recovery.

At times like this you'll find good reasons for giving up. Agoraphobia is a serpent, always whispering in your ear.

'All this is a lot of messing about. It takes up too much time,' it hisses.

'This can't be making me better because my panics have increased,' it reasons.

'What's so bad about the way I am? It's easier to leave things as they are,' it tempts.

'This isn't fair on my family. It's creating too much stress,' it coaxes.

All these arguments are plausible. Giving up is always the easier option. The Arctic explorer, lost and exhausted, knows that if he lies down in the snow and falls asleep he is dead. In the same way, the recovering agoraphobic must always fight the temptation to give up.

Never underestimate this temptation.

After all, like every agoraphobic, you're a master at talking yourself into trouble. In the past you've convinced yourself of the most implausible things. You've persuaded yourself that you'll go insane or drop down dead if you step inside a lift or walk into a busy supermarket.

Yet there is no basis for this in fact. In the annals of medical science you won't find a single case of an agoraphobic suffering any long-term ill effects from exposure to even the most dreaded situation.

How to overcome this negative self-talk is just one of the things this book will teach you. It is a vital part of a practical, holistic approach to tackling your phobia and its consequences.

This approach is reduced to a number of simple procedures, which ensure that you tackle your phobias in manageable stages. I assure you that if you follow these steps you will make steady progress.

ESCAPE!

Do not skip stages or rush ahead. Your condition did not occur in an instant nor will it disappear overnight. There is no shortcut to recovery.

But let me give two assurances.

None of the strategies I suggest can do you anything but good. They are all consistent with accepted medical opinion. As well as helping you overcome your phobias they will also improve your general health and well-being.

At the outset you may feel you do not have the courage to tackle a programme of recovery. Please, don't underestimate yourself. Phobics are courageous people. Those without phobias experience terror very seldom – if ever. You grapple with terror every day. Your determination to live a normal life is testimony to your courage.

Draw on that courage to carry you through to complete recovery.

Good luck.

Joseph O'Neill

ESCAPE!

CHAPTER 1
MY STORY – YOUR STORY

✓ My Story
✓ Your Story
✓ Action Points

Every agoraphobic's story is unique. Some trace the start of their problems back to a major life-altering event – a death in the family, illness or an accident. For others there is no clear beginning, just gradual changes until one day, for no apparent reason, terror grips them in what used to be an innocuous situation.

So what is the point in telling my story? What's so special about me?

Absolutely nothing. That is the point.

I've read many accounts by agoraphobics of the onset and development of their illness. Though each is different, they all describe four distinct phases in the development of their condition.

Recognising these phases is an important step in understanding how agoraphobia develops and how to recover.

The first phase begins when you have your first panic attack. Invariably, this appears from nowhere and is all the more terrifying for that.

The second phase is the result of how you react to panic. Misinterpreting what is happening to you is the key to this stage. You believe that panics will kill you, drive you insane or at the very least cause you to make an exhibition of yourself.

At the same time, you start to believe that what causes the panic is a particular situation. So, if you had your first panic attack in a lift, you develop a fear of lifts. If it was a supermarket, then you start to avoid big stores. But it doesn't stop there.

You start to generalise your apprehension. If your first attack was in a lift you start to feel anxious about other confined spaces – buses, trains, aeroplanes.

This gives rise to the third phase – avoidance behaviour. So that you do not have to risk having a panic attack, you shun the situations that might trigger it. You get your husband to do all the shopping, you take the stairs to the twenty-third floor and you stop taking continental holidays.

ESCAPE!

The final stage is the accommodation stage. Instead of confronting your difficulties and trying to resolve them, you build your life around them. You tell yourself that you don't go shopping because it's more convenient if other members of the family do it. You explain that you much prefer to holiday in England – you're bored with going abroad. It's good exercise, you explain, to climb stairs.

As you read my story, try to relate each of these phases to your own experience. Later you will write down the corresponding events in your story. This will help to identify the stage you are currently at and clarify the development of your condition.

But there's another reason for telling my story.

Thirty years ago, when I suffered my first panic attacks, I was certain I was going insane. Too ashamed to tell anyone what was happening to me, I was convinced that no one could understand what was I was suffering. I felt desperately alone.

This is a common reaction to the onset of agoraphobia, which is, however, extremely damaging, as it is a major obstacle to recovery. It is also completely untrue.

The truth is that agoraphobia is a common condition. Because so many sufferers conceal their illness and never seek help, it is impossible to know the exact number of agoraphobics. Some research suggests that as many as one in seventeen of the population suffer at some stage in their life. Others maintain that this is an exaggeration and that the figure is nearer to one in every one hundred and seventy.

Even if we accept the lower figure, there are about 350,000 agoraphobics in Britain. You are certainly not alone. There are certainly other agoraphobics among your colleagues, friends and acquaintances. You can be sure that many others are experiencing exactly what you are suffering.

ESCAPE!

MY STORY

I had my first panic attack in a lift. It was a wet Monday morning in March. I'd had a heavy weekend. At that time I often drank between eighteen and twenty pints of Guinness each night over the weekend. I was in bad shape in other ways too.

I was a heavy smoker. Many days I smoked two or three packets, between forty and sixty cigarettes. Looking back now I can see that when I did eat I ate a lot of the wrong things.

It was a time in my life when I was unhappy. I was in my second year at university and I felt completely aimless. This was in the late 'sixties, when the idea of a liberal education, without any specific vocational goal, still had some credibility. I was studying politics, history and philosophy and did not have a clue what I wanted to do when I graduated.

It was a turning point in my life. I'll discuss the nature panic attack fear later. For now, all I'll say is that no fear is like this fear. Some people claim that panic attack fear is the same as 'normal' fear, the sort of fear you experience when you are threatened or endangered. No one who has ever had a panic attack agrees.

If normal fear is like someone trying to scratch the paintwork of a car with his fingernails, phobic fear is like someone gouging it with a screwdriver. Panic fear scores the brain, leaving a lasting mark.

After the first attack I had a short reprieve. If it had only happened once I might have got over it. A week later it happened again.

I was sitting in a pub, laughing, when it struck. It was the last time I laughed for a long time.

From then on my whole life revolved around panic. An attack was unpleasant but what was worse was the fear of it. Fear stalked me wherever I went.

I stopped drinking. I avoided lifts first, then trains and buses. The attacks subsided. Respite became abeyance and then remission. But always there was the fear that it would recur. Even as the months passed I never felt secure – an attack could ambush me at any time.

Two years after my first attack, by which time I had graduated and was working, it happened again. I was under a great deal of stress at work and I felt at low ebb. This time they hit me like a volley of punches. I'd no sooner stumble out of one attack before another hit me. Their unpredictability was a new horror.

ESCAPE!

Every time I though I saw a pattern, it hit me from a new angle. At first I thought it was tiredness that sparked them. So I made an effort to get more rest. I'd go to bed early and wake more refreshed. This was the answer.

Until one morning, after a good night's sleep I woke with my stomach churning and heart racing, teetering on the verge of a panic. Just the thought of getting out of bed was enough to push me over the edge.

Each day was now a series of tightly packed crises. Life was closing in on me. I couldn't use public transport. I was terrified of being alone. I spent all day every day hovering on the edge of an attack. It couldn't go on.

I decided to go to the doctor.

It was the early 'seventies and Valium was the panacea. But it didn't work.

'Mother's little helpers come in many forms,' the psychiatrist assured me. So I worked my way through the spectrum of the pharmaceutical rainbow — Librium, Nobrium, diazepam — in ever-greater doses until I was totally hooked.

True, the attacks were no more. But in order not to feel anxiety I had given up feeling anything. I was living in a state of suspended animation. I was constantly tired, lethargic and uninterested in life. I never felt sad, but I never felt happy. Nothing touched me.

I know now that I was suffering the classic symptoms of benzodiazepine dependence. At the time it was a price I thought I was prepared to pay.

But then the symptoms that had caused me to take the medication in the first place started to reappear.

Depression and anxiety were reasserting themselves. An all-pervading dread clung to me like a weight strapped to my shoulder. I was always teetering on the edge of a panic attack. I become so preoccupied with it that nothing else fully engaged me. I so desperately wanted to avoid panic that the rest of my life was an afterthought.

Every aspect of life became an ordeal. It seemed that all my life consisted of was fear and dread.

Then there was the sense of unreality, the constant feeling of being thickheaded, as if I'd just woken after a drinking binge. My temper was always on a short fuse. My tolerance of any form of discomfort was low and it took very little to throw me into a rage.

My life was without purpose. My sole ambition was to get through the day without an attack. Surely tomorrow will be better, I'd tell myself. But it never is.

ESCAPE!

All the time I was searching for an explanation. It's because of the situation at work. When that changes I'll feel better. The situation at work changed. But I remained the same. In a world that presented new threats, impossible challenges every day, only one thing was constant: the sense of dread, the weight of foreboding.

My personality was changing. I was becoming totally egocentric. All that mattered was my state of mind, my need to avoid panic attacks. I was becoming totally self-absorbed, self –obsessed and lacking in consideration for others. My illness was making me ugly.

All this was taking a toll on my family, especially my saintly wife. Her tolerance and kindness knew no limit but even I was beginning to realise that she was entitled to more than a life as a nursemaid. I knew the situation could not continue. I had to do something.

I decided to do it my way. By now, in my thirties and into the 1980s, the age of self-help had dawned. I'd solve my own problems. Instead of studiously avoiding my problems, I would address them head-on.

First, I had to get off tranquillisers. I read everything on addiction. I drew up my own programme for tranquilliser withdrawal and coped with the symptoms. I practised relaxation techniques and started to confront my fears. I adopted the holistic approach. Someone suggested alcohol didn't help. I became tea-total. Nicotine and caffeine stimulate fear. I binned my cigarettes. Exercise helps, so I took up running, swimming and cycling. If nothing else I was going to be the healthiest agoraphobic in the world.

But although I felt immensely better I couldn't get to grips with the phobic situation.

Phobics are great rationalisers. 'Why do I need to use public transport? I've got a car.' ' I have no interest in foreign travel', I maintained. 'Why should I want to see the Hall of Mirrors when Blackpool is so near? What possible appeal could Rome hold when I can visit Morecambe?'

Besides, I had achieved a certain equilibrium. I felt better than I could ever remember. I no longer suffered panic attacks — provided I avoided the situations that sparked them. I convinced myself that my fears were like an innocuous scab: provided I didn't pick at them, they would eventually wither away.

But after a decade of being drug free, my fears were just as menacing. I had merely become more resourceful at circumnavigating them. I was chipping away at the edge of my problem, but the heart of it was still there, as solid as ever. I was in my forties and life was passing me by. I needed something to help me confront the heart of the problem. I found a psychiatrist in private practice.

ESCAPE!

Together we drew up a detailed hierarchy of my fears. Under hypnosis, I visualised myself totally relaxed in the first, least frightening phobic situation. Then I actually put myself into that situation over and over again until I could do it without fear. I then moved up the list tackling each phobia in the same way. It sounds so simple.

Like a demented bibliophile, I spent months going up and down in a library lift. Now the fear was diminishing. Eventually I graduated to more exotic lifts — departmental stores, office blocks, hotels — even the futuristic glass and steel affair in Bolton market hall.

I progressed to endless Sunday morning bus rides to Wigan and Leigh, weekends spent making interminable tram journeys from Alrincham to Bury, weekly train journeys to Birmingham enjoying the delights of Virgin travel. Occasionally I experienced the exquisite joy of boredom.

From the start I set myself a target: crossing the Channel. This became my ultimate goal, the measure of total recovery. We would visit friends in their French home.

Then I was ready for the first approximation to cross-Channel travel — the Mersey ferry. From the Pier Head to Seacombe and back via Woodside I went, time after time. The ticket seller and the crew, men of remarkable restraint, merely directed a quizzical glance at this devotee of what the boat's commentary called 'the most famous ferry in the world.' Eventually my galloping pulse slowed, the gasping eased and the cold sweat became a healthy glow. It was not for nothing my children had taken to calling me Captain Pugwash.

The prospect of crossing the Channel was now more than a distant hope. A date was fixed — 24 July. The long countdown was in its final phase.

Planning is as important to a phobic as to a bank robber. The unexpected is as welcome as a power-cut as you're being wheeled into the operating theatre. I researched and prepared every detail of the trip. We'd stay with friends in Maidenhead on the 23 and then, after a leisurely breakfast, drive on to Dover for the 11.45 ferry to Calais. From the start things went wrong.

We arrived at our friends at 2.00. pm. No one in. We waited. By 8 o'clock we realised there had been a mix up. Our plans were in tatters.

We decided to pressed on to Dover. It was the busiest time of the year for crossing to France and we were pessimistic about finding accommodation at eleven o'clock at night. We phoned friends who lived outside the town. They insisted on putting us up.

That sleepless night I could smell the sea and taste the salt. I rose early and, in the hope of burning off

ESCAPE!

the adrenalin coursing through my veins, went for a run on the South Downs. My legs could barely carry me. The soil was chalky, uneven and dry.

"Boarding in fifteen minutes, sir," she said, flashing a crisp smile and passing the tickets with bubblegum nails. "Lane 66, sir." The blood was thumping in my ears.

The avenue of roses in Coutances's famed botanical gardens is illuminated by uplighters. A tangle of scents fills the air. At the end of the avenue stands a gleaming monument to the French dead of a forgotten colonial war. An angel kisses the cold brow of a stricken soldier. Above an infinite expanse of sky is flecked with stars, winking in the cool night air.

YOUR STORY

Now answer the following questions on your experience. Put as much detail as possible into your answers.

1. When did you have your first panic attack? Describe the circumstances leading up to it in as much detail as possible. Write down all you can remember about the attack – where it happened, what you were doing, the time of day, everything you remember of it.

2. Think back to the time immediately after your first panic attack.
   a. What did you think was happening to you during that first panic attack?
   b. What did you fear would happen to you if you had another panic attack?
   c. What did you think was the way to avoid another panic attack?
   d. Were there other places you feared might spark a panic attack? If so, list them.
   e. List the places you started to avoid in the period after your first attack.

ESCAPE!

3. Note any other ways   in which your
    behaviour started to change. Were
    there things you stopped doing or
    things you started doing after the first
    attack? Were there any ways in which
    you started to feel differently?

4. Are there any ways in which you have
    started to make excuses for your
    changed behaviour by explaining it
    without referring to your fears?

Chapter 2

What is Agoraphobia?

➢ The need to know.
➢ What agoraphobia is not.
➢ Definition.
➢ Test your understanding.
➢ How agoraphobia starts and develops.
➢ Who becomes agoraphobic?
➢ The truth shall make you free.
➢ The origins of agoraphobia.
➢ What is happening?
➢ Learning to be agoraphobic.
➢ How we build a lifestyle around agoraphobia.
➢ Anxiety.
➢ The impact of agoraphobia on your life.
➢ What is really happening?
➢ Are you agoraphobic?
➢ Panic attacks.
➢ What is a panic attack?
➢ Checklist of symptoms.
➢ The development of panics.
➢ What is happening during a panic attack?

ESCAPE!

THE NEED TO KNOW

It was twenty-five years after I first presented to a doctor that my condition was correctly diagnosed. During that period I saw many doctors, several psychiatrists and a counsellor. Not one of them mentioned agoraphobia. In fact during that whole period I was offered nothing by way of explanation. There was nothing to stop my imagination conjuring up all sorts of terrifying explanations.

If you suffer from agoraphobia, you need to know. Otherwise it is impossible to successfully address the condition.

The first step is to define agoraphobia. A definition allows you to label your condition, to give it a name. But it doesn't tell you anything about the full impact it has on your life. But it is important to grasp this too if you are to fully appreciate the extent of the problem.

In particular, agoraphobia has a corrosive effect on confidence. This is one of its most significant effects because it locks you into the condition. Unless you appreciate your loss of confidence is a result of agoraphobia then it is extremely difficult to take those vital early steps towards recovery.

However, even defining agoraphobia is not easy. One reason for this is that agoraphobia is shrouded in misconceptions. These are so widespread and so damaging to sufferers that I shall deal with them first.

ESCAPE!

WHAT AGORAPHOBIA IS NOT

Neither agoraphobia nor any type of phobia is a mental illness. Nor is it a symptom of the onset of a nervous breakdown. As we shall see later, agoraphobia is the result of inappropriate learning. Nothing more than that. It is entirely wrong and harmful for an agoraphobic to think that he is going mad.

Another common misconception is that phobias are rare. I have already touched on this in Chapter 1 but as many agoraphobics feel isolated and ashamed because they do not realise how many others share their difficulties, it is important to reiterate this point. The most recent research indicates that about forty per cent of people suffer from some sort of phobia at some stage of their lives. One in ten people has a phobia that restricts their lifestyle. Agoraphobia is the commonest phobia and about 60% of phobics are agoraphobic.

Don't fool yourself. Having an anxiety-related problem doesn't make you special. A recent survey by the Health and Safety Executive found that 500,000 Britons suffer illness as a result of stress in the workplace.

American research tells a similar story. Between five and eight million people in the USA have a phobia severe enough to have a seriously disruptive effect on their mental health and daily functioning. There are estimated to be another fifteen to eighteen million whose phobic problem is more limited, affecting them significantly but not disrupting their lives so severely.

Many people believe, probably as the result of popular fiction and films, that agoraphobia is a fear of open spaces. As I will explain, this is only part of the condition. Most agoraphobics also suffer from fear of being confined. Additionally, they suffer from a more pervasive fear, what is called the fear of fear or the fear of panic.

Finally, it is important to understand that phobias cannot be conquered merely by will power. This idea arises because the non-phobic cannot understand that a lift or a crowded shop can be frightening. However, it is not only the non-phobic who falls for this "Snap out of it!" philosophy. Many phobics also convince themselves that by gritting their teeth and clenching their fists they can overcome their fears. All the evidence suggests that this simplistic approach just makes matters worse.

ESCAPE!

DEFINITION

The German psychologist, Dr. G. Westphal, was the first to use the term agoraphobia to describe a condition he had noticed in several patients who found it impossible to enter certain situations or could only do so with dread and anxiety.

As was the established medical convention in the nineteenth century Westphal named the condition with the Greek words 'agora' – market, marketplace, place of assembly and 'phobia' – meaning dread. Subsequently some people assumed that agoraphobia is simply "fear of open places."

The problem is that the 'open places' the agoraphobic fears take many different forms. What's more, he also fears confined spaces. But the range of situations that cause dread is more extensive even than this definition suggests. Agoraphobics commonly fear the following places:

- Streets
- Shops
- Shopping centres
- Bridges
- Motorways
- Cars
- Trains,
- Buses
- Lifts

- Tall buildings
- Heights of any kinds
- Classrooms
- Churches
- Theatres
- Parties
- Meeting halls
- Hairdressing chairs
- Dentists' chairs
- Waiting rooms
- Queues
- Rivers and lakes
- Car parks
- Mountains
- Sports stadiums
- Banks
- Launderettes
- Crowded areas
- Deserted places

Unrelated as these situations appear, they have something in common: the agoraphobic cannot make a rapid escape if something goes wrong. This is why he avoids them.

But what does he think might go wrong? He fears that he will have a panic attack and that if he cannot escape from the situation the attack will have dire consequences.

ESCAPE!

So what are these dreadful consequences, so dreadful that the mere possibility of them is enough to keep him from entering certain situations?

Some believe they will be struck down by a fatal condition, such as a heart attack. Others fear they will go insane while some feel they will make a fool of themselves and attract the derision of anyone who sees them.

In the hope of staying panic-free, agoraphobics avoid the feared situations. Unknown to them, however, this avoidance behaviour reinforces the fear of panic.

Even though agoraphobics initially manage to avoid panics by living restricted lives, for some even this is not enough. They find that even when they avoid phobic situations they are not free from panics.

For both, however, the need to avoid panics becomes an obsession.

TEST YOUR UNDERSTANDING (1)

Answer yes or no to each of these questions. Check your answers in the Appendix.

1. People who have panic attacks or agoraphobia are having a nervous breakdown.
2. The only problem for agoraphobics is that they can't stand open spaces.
3. Agoraphobics often avoid public transport.
4. All agoraphobics fear having a heart attack.
5. The best thing to do if you think you are developing agoraphobia is to stay away from places that frighten you.

ESCAPE!

HOW AGORAPHOBIA STARTS AND DEVELOPS

So far you have looked at the development of your condition and compared it with mine. Now I will outline the way the condition generally develops.

As you read through this section do what you did as you read through my story: compare it with your own experience.

Agoraphobia usually begins with a panic attack. (Panic attacks are such a key element of agoraphobia that Chapter 5 is devoted entirely to understanding and controlling them.)

For now you should know that a panic attack has two aspects – a set of thoughts and feelings, on the one hand and a set of physical reactions on the other.

The thoughts and feelings are overwhelming. The sufferer is certain that something terrible is happening and there is absolutely nothing he can do to control it. He may think that he is going to die, go insane or make an exhibition of himself. It seems that the only way to stop them is to escape to a place of safety.

Just as the mind is saying 'Run! Escape! Get out!' the body is preparing for flight. Muscles tense. The heart starts pounding. Breathing becomes rapid and shallow. This may result in a buzzing in the head or an intense feeling of unreality, as if you are outside yourself, viewing the situation from a distance. You break out in a cold sweat, your mouth dries up and it's difficult to swallow.

The first time this happened it seems to come completely out of the blue. As I will explain a little later, this is not usually the case.

Most agoraphobics trace the onset of their illness to a panic attack. The instinctive reaction to panic is flight so most people rush away – anywhere as long as it is somewhere else. If it happened in a lift, he got out at the next floor. If it happened in a supermarket he made for the nearest door. If on a train he got off at the next station.

As soon as he escapes fear starts to drain away. The racing heart slows, breathing begins to return to normal, the stomach stops churning, the morbid thoughts disappear.

This first attack is traumatic. Even one panic attack is a shattering blow to confidence. It leaves a profound sense of insecurity.

At some stage after this terrifying experience he convinces himself that should he again enter the situation in which he panicked, the same thing will happen.

ESCAPE!

Looking back on that first panic it seems even worse than it really was. Not understanding what was happening, he imagined all sorts of terrible things were going on in his mind and body.

He draws a fateful conclusion: he must avoid the place where he suffered his first attack or else face horrendous consequences. He is convinced that having another panic attack is just about the worst thing that could possibly happen.

But this is only the beginning. Staying away from the supermarket is not enough to avoid attacks. After a while he starts wondering about other crowded places. What about shopping malls, concert halls, theatres and sports stadiums where he might find himself packed in with other people? 'They're just as bad as the supermarket,' he reasons. 'I'd better avoid them too.'

Before long there are many places and situations he fears.

Perhaps something else happens. Perhaps he manages to avoid all these places and still has an attack. Maybe it happens when he is in the safety of his own home.

Now nowhere is safe.

His world starts to shrink in proportion to his loss of confidence. Sometimes it becomes impossible to leave home without the support of a friend.

Sometimes even this is not enough and he is confined within four walls.

But often he makes his isolation worse. Most people who suffer panic attacks are too ashamed to tell friends or family. They fear they will not understand or may even misinterpret the symptoms as signs of insanity.

Perhaps he tells his doctor. Maybe he takes medication or sees a counsellor. This may have helped but it does not cure the underlying problem.

Meanwhile his life continues to contract. There are more and more places he avoids. It limits his social life. It may even create problems at work. Soon it starts to impinge on his family as he finds it difficult to travel and doesn't want to be left alone or out of reach of a friend.

And other fears are flourishing all the time. Those situations that elicit mild anxiety in most people – visiting the dentist, job interviews, speaking in public – become major ordeals. All this starts to get him down. Over 70% of those who suffer from agoraphobia report that throughout the course of the disorder they have experienced intermittent spells of depression.

It's easy to see how agoraphobia can lead to isolation and loneliness, especially when it makes

ESCAPE!

it impossible to hold down a job and reduces social contacts outside the home.

When agoraphobia leads to the loss of full-time employment this invariably creates a whole raft of financial and marital stresses as well.

However, a surprisingly large number of men do manage to maintain their jobs while suffering from agoraphobia. Women find it more difficult. Perhaps this is because there is more social pressure on men to stay in employment.

Yet even if he manages to hold down a job he often feels ashamed and starts to think of himself as inadequate or worthless. He may feel guilty about the impact of his illness on those close to him, especially when they start to organise their lives around his fears. As time goes on and his condition becomes an accepted part of his life he may come to believe that things will never improve and that he has to accept agoraphobia as his lot in life.

Resignation of this sort has some apparent advantages. Once your family has accepted that you do not go shopping, then the weekly journey to the supermarket is someone else's responsibility. If you have to give up work because you cannot leave home, then you avoid the stress that is part of every job. Because you don't do parties, you have to reluctantly forego the pleasure of your mother-in-law's fascinating get-together and the joy of her vegetarian canapés.

The problem with these advantages is that they are poisonous sweets. They reinforce the condition. This is not to say that the agoraphobic does not want to get better or that he is happy to remain ill. But like every ill wind, agoraphobia has a pay-off.

And the kinder and more considerate friends and family are, the more harm they cause. (Later on I will explain how you can enlist a helper who, by fulfilling a specific role, can support you through recovery.) This is because sympathy often accommodates the pattern of avoidance that is developing and which reinforces phobic fears.

Even if he sought medical advice there is every possibility his condition was misdiagnosed and the treatment he received was inappropriate.

All this adds to the agoraphobic's general level of anxiety. Before long anxiety and stress are an habitual condition. This, in turn, leads to physical changes including a tensing of muscles often resulting in symptoms, usually painful cramps, commonly in the neck or stomach. Often the sufferer is convinced he is physically ill.

Along with these bodily changes, he generally develops certain assumptions about his condition.

ESCAPE!

As these have such an impact on the condition it is important to examine them.

'I'm the most unfortunate person in the world.'

Many agoraphobics fall victim to self-pity. Snared by an incomprehensible illness that seems to poison every aspect of life it is easy to feel that you are the most unfortunate person in the world. Self-pity of the moping, hopeless and despairing variety is harmful. It can easily become a justification for doing nothing. 'I'm cursed with this condition and there's nothing I can do about it.' This is simply not true, as I shall prove. Instead of wasting your energy railing against fate, channel your anger into recovery.

'I cannot tolerate any anxiety'

People who suffer panic attacks quickly become obsessed with their condition. They develop the habit of scanning their bodies and monitoring their feelings for the early warning signs of an attack. Consequently, they develop a heightened sensitivity to anxiety. Any of the symptoms associated with an attack – an increased pulse rate, a dry mouth, perspiration – may now trigger panic. In trying to protect himself against panic the agoraphobic is bringing on the very thing he fears.

'I'm going crazy.'

In the absence of a correct diagnosis this is the sort of assumption the agoraphobic is likely to make. Even though it is a wrong assumption, it nevertheless adds to the distress and fear and increases the general level of anxiety.

'People think I'm weird.'

Phobics tend to be sensitive about what other people think of them and to imagine that everyone is critical of their behaviour. One of the phobic's greatest fears is that he will do something embarrassing. In fact, people are no more interested in or critical of the phobic's behaviour than they are in anyone else's. Most people are concerned with themselves and if they do notice someone is distressed they are likely to be helpful rather than mocking. Besides, panic attacks do not cause people to run amok or do anything likely to attract attention.

ESCAPE!

WHO BECOMES AGORAPHOBIC?

Many agoraphobics become obsessively interested in the origins of their condition, thinking it might hold the key to recovery. Many believe it might be the result of background or personality.

Agoraphobics come from all walks of life. They are found in all age groups and in every strata of society. There is no social or psychological profile of the 'agoraphobic type.'

However, research suggests that many agoraphobics share certain traits and attitudes. Whether or not these contribute to the development of agoraphobia is not clear. However, these traits are important because many of them are invaluable skills that can be used to aid recovery.

Most agoraphobics are highly imaginative and can remember being so as children. The disadvantage of this is that it enables them to recall in great detail and with intense emotional force the situations that they find so painful. On the other hand a powerful imagination is a great asset in many of the visualisation strategies I will introduce later. The more convincingly you are able to visualise yourself anxiety-free in phobic situations the easier it will be to enter that situation.

Agoraphobics tend to underrate their value and capabilities. Their estimation of themselves is generally modest. This tendency, if allowed to go unchecked can lead to a poor self-image and a lack of confidence. As you will see, part of the recovery strategy involves challenging your negative self-image and adopting a more realistic assessment of your capabilities.

At the same time many agoraphobics set high and unrealistic goals for themselves and worry about failing. What is even more stressful is that they often allow others to set demanding goals for them and strive to live up to their expectations. This leads to a great deal of stress. What makes it worse is that many agoraphobics are over conscientious in the performance of duties and obligations. They are often perfectionists and regard anything less than total success as a disaster.

Because agoraphobics tend to be overly sensitive to what others think of them they are often 'people-pleasers.' They worry about others having a poor opinion of them, so they conceal their condition from others because they fear being though crazy or weird. Obviously this need for secrecy creates an additional problem, an added difficulty and at the same time confirms their suspicion that their condition is dreadful. Removing this need for secrecy is part of the recovery process.

ESCAPE!

So far I've discussed how the agoraphobic sees his situation. A big part of the problem is that this perception is wrong. The best antidote to this distorted perception is the truth. A vital early step on the road to recovery requires the agoraphobic to understand the reality of his situation and see it for what it really is – not what he imagines it to be.

CHECK YOUR CHARACTERISTICS

Rate yourself for each of the traits listed below. Five is the highest level and one the lowest.

Imaginative:1   2   3   4   5
Positive self-image: 1   2   3   4   5
Set myself high standards: 1   2   3   4   5
Keep my condition secret: 1   2   3   4   5

ESCAPE!

CAUSES OF AGORAPHOBIA

Knowledge about the causes of agoraphobia may be helpful but it is not essential for recovery. The particular situation that sparked your agoraphobia makes no difference to what is required to recover. It is, however, worth considering the onset of your condition to remove some of the fear and misunderstanding that plays such a big part in sustaining agoraphobia.

Most sufferers seem to think that agoraphobia sprang out of nowhere. This is one of the reasons why it is so frightening: it gives no warning. Everything is going along as normal and then suddenly you are gripped by this terrible disability.

It may seem this way, but usually there is more to it. Often the warning signs were there, but they went unnoticed. It could well have been when you faced a major life change. This is why it generally occurs between the ages of seventeen and thirty-five, the period when most of are undergoing life's major transitions.

It generally happens when new fears challenge our security. Many people report that their first attack happened when they were about to enter into a serious commitment. Taking on a new job with additional responsibilities, moving out of your parents' home, setting up on one's own, the break-up of a close relationship, or the serious illness or death of someone close are all situations associated with the start of agoraphobia.

Relationship problems create stress and tension that builds over a long period. Marital breakdown or problems with children often create this situation. Disagreements with in-laws or responsibility for the care of an elderly or dependent relation can also create strain.

Marital quarrels too can be as potent as an actual break-up in producing the sort of intense, chronic anxiety out of which a phobic reaction may erupt. This may have built up over a period of time, so gradually that it has gone unnoticed. Where a specific problem is the cause of stress it may well have arisen some time before the symptoms of agoraphobia showed themselves, but usually within the previous year.

Major life transitions are also fraught with difficulties. Retirement, marriage, a prison sentence, moving house and changing job all make great demands on our ability to adapt to challenging circumstances. Problems at work or financial difficulties often lead to dissatisfaction and worry that spills into every area of life.

The use of illegal drugs is commonly a factor in the onset of agoraphobia. Many medical practitioners believe that about one in ten agoraphobics first suffered symptoms immediately after or while under the influence of non-prescription drugs.

Generally the more transitions we are going through at any one time, the greater the stress. Even welcome changes – a marital reconciliation, promotion, the arrival of a baby, even a financial windfall – involve stress.

Others link the onset of their condition to a time when their resistance was low. Perhaps this was because of illness or while suffering an infection. Many women cite immediately after childbirth as the time when symptoms first appeared.

Others link the condition to a period in their lives when they felt powerless. This may be because they feel trapped in an unhappy marriage, a frustrating job, a narrow social life or by a dominating parent or partner.

It may seem as if agoraphobia came out of nowhere but usually it appears against a background of long-standing stress. Claire Weekes maintains that physical illness is the commonest background.

What is really happening?

Apart from reflex reactions like the knee jerk, we learn all our behaviour just as we learnt to read and write and talk. It is only by looking back that we remember how skills, which now seem automatic – like riding a bike or driving a car – were once acquired only by means of an arduous learning process.

Psychologists now see lots of our behaviour in this way. They talk about the situation in which we find ourselves as the stimulus and the way we react as the response.

Sometimes the way this works is obvious, as when we are near food. Automatically, we start to salivate. Research shows the most effective way to teach a particular behaviour is by immediately giving a reward every time that behaviour is carried out. These rewards are of two types, positive and negative.

The first, the positive reinforcement, the pleasant consequence of our action, make us want to repeat that action. So, the reason we look forward to that ice cream the waiter is bringing over to our table is because we remember with delight our last ice cream. Secondly there are negative reinforcements – the removal of an unpleasant situation following the performance of a piece of behaviour. So the reason we keep our hand out of the fire is because of the pain we felt when we were last burnt and the memory of how the pain lessened when you removed it from the heat.

Any behaviour that is followed by one or the other of these rewarding consequences is likely to become established. It is important however, that

ESCAPE!

the reinforcement occur instantly after the behaviour. Otherwise it will have no effect on establishing that response in the future. So, if you wish to encourage your son to continue completing his homework before seven o'clock, you must give him the bar of chocolate immediately after he has crossed the last 't'. To fully reinforce the message, on those evening when he doesn't meet the deadline, you should send him to his bedroom on the stroke of seven. If you give him the reward several days later it will not have the same impact in encouraging him to become studious. Likewise, if you he failed to do his homework on a Monday, sending him to bed early at the weekend is less effective.

LEARNING TO BE AGORAPHOBIC

In exactly the same way we learn to be agoraphobic.

The first time we felt anxiety in a particular situation, we fled. Thereafter we avoided the situation. We escaped fear by flight and then kept it at bay by avoidance.

Fleeing gives an immediate and powerful sense of relief. This is a potent reinforcement of our action, making it likely that if we ever again find ourselves in that situation again, we will want to flee.

Thereafter we resorted to avoidance. Each time we do this we get an immediate reward – a release from the dread entering the phobic situation. This is the perfect negative reinforcement. And as this negative reinforcement is so powerful it becomes the way in which we deal with frightening situations – we avoid them. At first this might apply only to the situation in which you had your first panic attack. Soon, however, you apply it to anywhere you fear might cause an attack. Avoidance becomes a way of life.

But something equally harmful is happening at the same time. You are going through a process of sensitisation. What this means is that your

ESCAPE!

nervous and emotional responses are becoming more and more powerful. In other words, the fear you have of entering the phobic situation is becoming greater and greater. At the same time panic now appears more quickly than ever before. Now you get more scared more quickly. The fear response is now on a hair trigger.

This increasing tendency to feel intense fear is one of the major reasons why we make sure we avoid the phobic situation and anywhere else we feel panic might strike.

Even this, however, is not all.

At the same time your general background level of tension increases. Nervous tension is a constant, stress and anxiety are permanent conditions.

All this arises from the way you react to the phobic situation. If you are to unlearn your fear reaction, you must return to that situation and gradually learn to react in a different way.

HOW WEBUILD A LIFESTYLE AROUND AGORAPHOBIA

Phobics are very creative. They are ingenious at inventing explanations for irrational behaviour. These serve to justify their conduct both to the outside world and themselves. Often this justification becomes so firmly entrenched that they have no sense of acting in an irrational way. Because their families and friends are generally sympathetic they try to shield them from the anxiety of confronting their fears. In most cases this collusion is a significant factor in the establishment of a phobia because all avoidance reinforces the phobic response. Despite their good motives, by supporting avoidance behaviour, family and friends are making things more difficult in the long run.

Justification and collusion obscure the basic problems and construct a lifestyle that allows agoraphobia to grow unchecked. What's worse, they restrict not only the phobic's life but also that of those around him – sometimes to a crippling extent.

ESCAPE!

ANXIETY

What holds all this together is fear. Like the strings that hold a marionette's limbs in place, fear gives agoraphobia its shape and form. It is therefore vital that we understand how fear arises and how it functions. Otherwise a lot of what follows in later chapters about disarming and controlling fear will make no sense.

When confronted with what we see as a threatening situation we have the choice of fleeing or confronting the danger. Our bodies are hardwired to respond to this threat by preparing us for fight or flight. Our blood starts to pump with increased speed to supply energy to the muscles and the brain. This diverts blood away from certain areas of the body, especially the gut.

To increase the amount of oxygen in the blood and the speed with which carbon dioxide, the by-product of rapid muscular action, is drawn away, the rate of respiration is stepped up. Digestion is suspended and the supply of saliva is reduced. Sweating increases to keep the body cool during this period of intense activity. Heart rate and blood pressure increase, our breathing speeds up, we become pale as blood drains from the skin, our stomachs churn and our mouths become dry.

All this happens not because of any decision made by the thinking part of the brain but by the specialist, self-regulating survival mechanism known as the autonomic nervous system. At the same time fear triggers glandular secretions. One of the most powerful of these is a spurt of adrenaline, which causes a surge of anxiety.

The autonomic nervous system sends orders through a network of nerve fibres, which are divided into two branches: the sympathetic branch and the parasympathetic branch. The sympathetic is energy expanding and the parasympathetic is energy conserving. One orders the body to get going and the other orders it to slow down.

The nervous system is like the body's automatic pilot – it switches the body into survival mode when we are threatened. As soon as the danger passes, the parasympathetic branch of the autonomic nervous system regains the upper hand. It reduces the heart rate and the blood pressure, restores digestion, returns the blood to the skin, limits the amount of perspiration being produced and slows down respiration. After a while the symptoms of anxiety disappear.

This happens much faster if the fear results in a burst of strenuous activity that burns up the excess adrenaline in the bloodstream.

ESCAPE!

THE IMPACT OF AGORAPHOBIA ON YOUR LIFE

But agoraphobia is not a problem confined to panic attacks. It affects every aspect of life, colouring your whole outlook.

Much of this is because agoraphobics are particularly suggestible to threatening ideas. They are often preoccupied with morbid thoughts and the mere suggestion of anything sad or depressing often fills them with apprehension. This pervasive gloom and despondency is a major reason why many agoraphobics feel they will never recover. It makes the temptation to give up the so powerful. It is all part of the loss of confidence that makes you so susceptible to negative thoughts that are a counsel of despair. This is why a programme of desensitisation is vital if you are to regain your confidence.

Agoraphobics also tend to become indecisive. They find it very difficult to make even trivial decisions. This can lead to a tendency to let things drift. Instead of making a decision and determining the course of their lives they often make no decision and allow events to take their own course. This in turn increases the feeling of not being in control of events.

Agoraphobics are also prone to intense introspection, anxious self-scrutiny and self-obsession. The result for about four out of ten agoraphobics is the feeling that they are somehow cut off from or are far out of touch with their surroundings. One sufferer described this condition as like being wrapped in Clingfilm. It's as if their ears are stuffed with cotton wool and they hear only a distant muffled sound without any edge to it. Another says it is like watching people on a television without sound. It's difficult to relate to others, to feel anything for them or to accept that they too experience emotions.

This deadpan emotional state in which the only feeling is fear is extremely disconcerting. Among other things it often gives rise to guilt because agoraphobics often feel they cannot experience love for those close to them. It is as if their obsession with fear has made them incapable of feeling any other emotion.

This experience may last for only a few minutes or go on for days and weeks. Fortunately it is one of the first symptoms to lift as you gain understanding of your condition and your obsessive introspection eases.

ESCAPE!

WHAT IS ACTUALLY HAPPENIING WITH AGORAPHOBIA?

For the agoraphobic the danger is not something he sees outside himself – it is the feelings or emotions of fear that he dreads. He is totally convinced that a panic attack is the worst thing that could happen to him and that it will do him serious damage. Whatever the price, he must avoid it.

The result is that he becomes obsessed with detecting the minute bodily changes that might signal the onset of a panic attack. He constantly scans his body looking for the slightest changes.

Of course, our bodies and our thoughts are in a constant state of flux. They change all the time depending on what we are doing. When we walk up stairs, our heart speeds up. When we go into a crowded room we feel warmer. When we cut the lawn we pant slightly.

Most people are largely unaware of these changes. They aren't important and if they do notice them, as they attach no significance to them, they quickly forget them.

But for the agoraphobic, these are danger signals, possibly the beginnings of a panic. Soon he becomes obsessed with spotting these alarm signals. His attention becomes turned in on himself. Every shift of feeling, every change of bodily tempo is a potential threat.

This constant state of anticipation becomes more and more acute and leads to a permanent state of anxiety. If you are constantly asking yourself, 'Is this the start of an attack?' the inevitable result is a state of heightened tension.

What's more, this constant anticipation of disaster is a form of self-hypnosis. You are making panic more likely, because you are telling yourself that at any time you may have a devastating attack and there is nothing you can do about it. It's no wonder you feel bad. It's just like someone walking around with an Ipod that plays the same message over and over again into his ears –' Watch out, there's a mugger stalking you!' Is it any wonder he feels anxious?

The agoraphobic lives in a hell or fear. Now he has his own mobile phobia. It can strike anywhere – any time. There's no escape.

ESCAPE!

ARE YOU AGORAPHOBIC?

Checklist of Symptoms

Tick or cross the following symptoms

- ✓ Frightened of confined spaces.
- ✓ Frightened of being in places from which you cannot easily escape.
- ✓ Frightened of being among crowds from which you cannot easily escape.
- ✓ Frightened of being alone or separated from a significant other (partner, family member or friend, who knows your fears and supports you).
- ✓ Frightened of travelling in a vehicle (bus, train, aircraft) over which you do not have control
- ✓ Frightened of having a panic attack

The more of these symptoms you have, the more likely it is that you are suffering from agoraphobia. If you have four or more of these symptoms then there is little doubt that you are agoraphobic.

PANIC ATTACKS

For most sufferers the panic attack is the doorway to agoraphobia. Understanding what is happening when you have an attack is an essential step to recovery.

What is a Panic Attack?

No two people's attacks are the same. For these reasons it is difficult to say precisely what a panic attack involves.

In 1980 the American Psychiatric Association defined panic attacks in their Diagnostic and Statistical Manual. This states that the following thirteen sensations are the main ones that occur during a panic attack.

1. A sense of dreamlike unreality or 'depersonalisation'.

2. Dizziness, unsteadiness or faintness
3. Pounding heart
4. Gasping for breathe or smothering sensation.
5. Trembling or shaking
6. Sweating
7. Choking
8. Nauseous or nervous tummy
9. Numbness or tingling sensation especially in the hands or legs

ESCAPE!

10. Hot flushes
11. Chest pains or discomfort
12. Acute fear of dying,
13. Acute fear of going insane or 'making an exhibition' of yourself.

CHECKLIST OF SYMPTOMS

Look back over the list of symptoms above. Tick or cross them.

Count up your ticks.

To qualify as a panic attack

- Any four of these symptoms must be present
- They have to start suddenly and unexpectedly
- They must become severe within a ten minute period
- There should be no obvious threatening situation setting them off.
- There should be no illness or disease responsible for these symptoms.

These thirteen symptoms are only the main ones and there are several others, which are quite common. These include a compulsion to run, the sensation of a great surge of fear, intense dread and a powerful sense of impending doom.

However, no matter how detailed, a list of symptoms does nothing to convey the overwhelming terror that is the reality of a panic attack. A severe panic attack shakes you to the core. One sufferer said that afterwards he felt as if he had been run-over by a racing car and could not quite believe he was still intact.

It is also important to remember that panic fear is a unique type of fear. Anyone who has had a panic attack will tell you that what they experience is terror, more intense than any fear.

ESCAPE!

THE DEVELOPMENT OF PANIC

The first attack seems to come out of the blue, for no apparent reason. This is one of the reasons why it is so frightening. It is usually followed by others a short time after and then becomes a regular feature of life.

Often the attack is associated with a particular place – such as a crowded shop. There is often some element of being confined or trapped in the situation – a room from which escape is difficult or can only be achieved with embarrassing explanations – such as a doctor or dentist's waiting room.

For many people it begins with uncontrollable physical sensations. This is one of the reasons why many agoraphobics cannot tolerate any substance – alcohol, cigarettes or drugs – that induces feelings which they cannot control. Many agoraphobics become terrified of flu because the symptoms, particularly the woozy, light-headed sensation of being distant from your surroundings, mimic those of panic.

They become obsessed with their next attack. In the phobic's mind this next attack is going to be the worst of all. It will go on longer, be more intense and more damaging. He feels that the next time he may not come out of it. No matter how long between attacks, the phobic is certain that the next attack is just around the corner, as inevitable as death. No matter how enjoyable leisure activities promise to be there is always the possibility that lurking in the folds of pleasure is the terror of an attack.

It is this fear of being caught out by a panic attack when away from home that restricts the agoraphobic's movements. His world is constantly shrinking. Nothing contributes more to this than the realisation that even a thought can spark the onset of an attack. Even thinking about a panic attack can induce one. Some people find that it creeps up on them when they should be most relaxed – when they are dropping off to sleep. They lurch wide-awake bathed in sweat. Or sometimes they wake up feeling paralysed by fear.

Panic is a portable phobia.

Once the agoraphobic detects any of the alarm symptoms he thinks, 'Oh my God! It's starting again!' This self-talk increases the fear and this in turn results boost the physical symptoms – breathing becomes even quicker and more ragged and pulse rate increases. This in turn increases the negative thoughts. ' It's definitely starting. I can't get my breath.'

This in turn leads to further avoidance of the situation where the panic arose – which can eventually become total.

ESCAPE!

WHAT IS ACTUALLY HAPPENING DURING A PANIC ATTACK?

To summarise this section, it is clear that panic consists of two elements: a set of physical symptom (3 – 11 in the checklist above) and a set of thoughts (1,2,12 & 13 in the checklist).

What the sufferer does not realise is that though panic mounts to a level where it seems it simply cannot be tolerated, it does not remain at that level for long. It begins to recede. It may rise again briefly but once it has peaked it inevitably declines.

Nor does he appreciate that the distress he feels in the course of a panic fluctuates. Looking back he remembers only the terror. But in fact it gets worse as he concentrates on and reacts automatically to the dangers he perceives in the phobic situation –the frightening thoughts and images of what can happen to him. It gets better as he shifts his attention away from those things onto other, reassuring things.

These facts – that you can learn to control the level of panic and that when it peaks panic automatically declines – are the key to mastering fear. As you will see in Chapter 5, they enable us to control our fear.

This is wonderful news for the agoraphobic. What is even better is that psychiatrists have developed a number of proven techniques that mean agoraphobics can use their control over fear to remove all those restrictions that limit their lives. I'll explain how these work in the next chapter.

CHAPTER 3   What Therapies are Available?

AVAILABLE THERAPIES

During my years as an agoraphobic I sampled all mainstream and many alternative therapies. Some were effective, others, at best, a waste of time.

In this short chapter I discuss the major therapies, emphasising those that are proven to be effective. These are the ones that make up the therapy I recommend. It is therefore important that you understand both the thinking that underpins them and how they relate to each other.

I also touch on two therapies – drug and psychoanalysis – that I do not recommend. This too is necessary because both were once widely used and many people reading this will want to know if there is anything to recommend them.

DRUG THERAPY

Drugs such as Valium and Librium (and other Benzodiazepines) reduce anxiety and make it easier to tolerate the phobic situation. Consequently these were once widely prescribed to agoraphobics. However, though this type of medication was never designed for long-term use, many agoraphobics took them for years, with unfortunate consequences.

Benzodiazapines do nothing to eliminate the root problem nor do they provide any lasting anxiety control. What's more, there is a great deal of evidence to suggest that long-term use eventually intensifies the problems for which they were originally prescribed.

If you are currently taking this type of medication you should discuss the matter with your GP. Do not discontinue prescribed drugs without first consulting your doctor.

PSYCHOANALYSIS

According to Sigmund Freud, the founder of psychoanalysis, all phobias have the same basic origins – they are the result of a repressed wish, desire, fear, hatred or other emotion. These emotions are directed away from the original object that gave rise to them and projected onto another, innocuous object; which becomes the object of dread. For instance, a man may develop agoraphobia because of his childhood fear that by leaving home he was abandoning his mother to his father.

In treating the condition the Freudian therapist helps the patient to uncover the repressed emotions, to confront them and to recognise that they are not bad or immoral. Once the patient understands these emotions the symptoms should disappear.

But even Freud acknowledged that the patient still has to confront the phobic situation to overcome his dread.

This form of treatment was once widely used but it is now acknowledged among those treating agoraphobia that psychoanalysis is not the most effective therapy.

CONDITIONING OR LEARNING THERAPY

This treatment is based on the belief that at the core of every emotional disorder – anxiety, depression, obsessive compulsive disorder, phobias – is a system of wrong ideas and beliefs the sufferer has about himself and the world in which he lives. In the case of the phobic his groundless fears are what he thinks could happen to him in the phobic situation.

Cognitive therapy – another name for this approach – uses many different techniques but essentially they all help the patient to

- work out exactly what he thinks might happen in the phobic situation
- understand that this is a thought not a fact or a reality
- test these false thoughts against reality to prove they are not correct and
- as a result of this experience, change his thinking about the phobic situation.
  This treatment has also been extremely successful in helping those suffering from depression. However, effective though it is, it is not usually used on its own but together with behavioural therapy. This combination has proved more effective than either on its own.

HYPNOSIS

ESCAPE!

Despite all the mystique surrounding hypnosis, particularly as used by entertainers, it is basically very simple. It involves a person who is in a relaxed and receptive state receiving suggestions about his future feelings and actions – what is called a post-hypnotic suggestion.

Psychiatrists and psychologists sometimes use hypnosis in the treatment of phobias, usually together with other methods. It is particularly helpful in preparing people to enter the phobic situation and once there, to control their anxiety.

Self-hypnosis is now a well-established means of changing undesirable behaviour. It is widely used by professional athletes and others who perform under great pressure. It is of great value to the agoraphobic, and is particularly useful when combined with cognitive and behavioural therapy.

In Chapter 9 I shall explain how you can use self-hypnosis in exactly the same way as psychiatrists use it to prepare for entering the phobic situation and, once there, to control your anxiety.

BEHAVIOURAL THERAPY

This is simplest form of therapy. In recent decades it has proved so much more effective than other treatments that it is now the most widely used therapy.

As we saw, Freud puts forward an elaborate explanation for the origin of phobias. The treatment he proposed involves a psychiatrist spending a great deal of time delving into the patient's subconscious mind to uncover the root of the condition. Behavioural therapy, on the other hand, is not really concerned with what causes agoraphobia.

Instead it offers a cure, which often produces rapid results. It teaches the sufferer to confront the situations that trigger anxiety and to cope with the fear. By repeating this over a period of time the intensity and duration of the anxiety tapers off until it eventually disappears. In effect, the sufferer gets used to the situation.

Put this another way. This school of psychology holds that phobias develop through a process of conditioning or learning and that we recondition or relearn through exposing ourselves to the phobic situation.

This form of treatment has, however, become a victim of its own success. There is such demand for it that the agencies providing it are overwhelmed. Waiting lists are long.

Even after the agoraphobic has waited months, perhaps years, and at last gets to see a medical health professional, his problems are not at an end. If, as is likely, he is prescribed a programme based mainly on behavioural principles, the onus for carrying out the programme is very much on the patient. The psychiatrist will devise a list of the situations he has to confront and a strategy for tackling them. What he will not do is accompany him each time he confronts the phobic situation.

BENEFITS OF SELF-HELP

This is why self-help is so important. Essentially, any effective recovery programme is a self-help programme. There is no alternative.

Nor is this a bad thing. Isaac M Marks, a leader in the treatment of phobias, says. "In my practice I find that the great majority of the depressed patients referred to me improve substantially if they try to help themselves. Sometimes it hardly seems to matter what you do as long as you do something with the attitude of self-help."

The programme I propose does not involve drug therapy or psychoanalysis. It draws on all the other therapies outlined and combines them in such a way as to derive the optimum benefit from each. Between them, they cover every facet of recovery.

Each element of the programme is widely used by professionals in this field. None is contrary to current medical practice and none can do you any harm.

There are two prongs to the approach I advocate. The first is directed at reducing your general everyday level of anxiety. The more relaxed and anxiety-free you are, the less likely you are to suffer from panic attacks.

The second prong is directed at changing how you react in the phobic situation. This is the key to recovery. It enables you to gradually enter the phobic situation in a structured and manageable way so that you are able to control your anxiety and eventually eliminate it.

These two prongs are complementary. If you plunge into the phobic situation in a state of high anxiety you will inevitably panic. If however, you first reduce your level of anxiety and then gradually enter the phobic situation in manageable stages, armed with strategies for controlling your panic, you learn to cope. By repeating this over and over again you gain mastery over your anxiety.

The fears that now limit your life disappear.

ESCAPE!

WHAT IT TAKES TO SUCCEED

Many agoraphobics regard themselves as victims. Perhaps you have suffered for many years. You may even have tried several forms of treatment, often drug based, and made no progress. Such experiences may blind you to the fact that your condition is curable and the means of recovery are at hand. All you have to do is embrace them and commit yourself to doing what is necessary to recover.

Before you can do that, however, you have to acknowledge the full impact of agoraphobia on your life. Not all of its effects are entirely negative. Some may be so pleasant that it is hard to give them up. This is one of the things I found most difficult to accept.

Having agoraphobia may guarantee attention from your spouse, children, friends and neighbours. It may mean that you do not have to face up to unpleasant things – you have a ready-made excuse for not going where you don't want to go. Perhaps it means that you don't work. Certainly, this may cause major financial problems. But it saves you from the stress of full-time employment. It means you don't have to fight your way through the rush-hour traffic or endure the nine-to-five grind.

Long-term agoraphobics organise every aspect of their lives to avoid anxiety. They feel this is imposed on them. This may be so, but not all aspects of their restricted lives are unpleasant.

You have to be honest with yourself about your current lifestyle and acknowledge the positive aspects. Because these too will have to change if you are to recover fully.

In some ways, these aspects of the condition are the most insidious. If these benefits prevent you from making a wholehearted commitment to recovery, they will become the seal locking you into your illness.

None of this is intended to minimise the problems of agoraphobia – merely to point out that they are not always obvious.

This is not surprising. Agoraphobia is so difficult to overcome precisely because the problems it creates are wide-ranging and deeply established. This is also why setbacks are an inevitable part of recovery.

To reduce the impact of setbacks and help you to stay on course, enlist a helper. Among other things a helper gives you the opportunity to discuss your position openly and provides perspective on your condition. This is something I'll return to later.

ESCAPE!

MAKING A COMMITMENT TO RECOVER

If you are to make a complete recovery and lead a full, unrestricted life you must accept and commit to the following:

1. This programme is open-ended. There is no time limit. This is because you proceed at your own pace. You must fully understand and practice each stage of the programme before advancing to the next stage. You must therefore commit yourself to following it for as long as it takes. No one can specify how long each stage will take. It all depends on your condition and your commitment. What is certain is that the more conscientiously you practice the greater your progress.

   Consequently, you must commit to working at this programme for as long as it takes.

2. To carry out this programme you must allocate a certain amount of time each day to reducing your level of anxiety and confronting the phobic situation. Do not make excuses for not practising. If you have to miss a session then don't worry – just carry on from where you left off. If you miss several sessions, you must go back over some of the stages you completed before the break in practice.

Consequently, you must commit to allocating the necessary time each week to work through this programme.

3. Many phobics put off tackling their problem because they are worried about the degree of stress involved. Sometimes this is because they have heard of a type of therapy called "flooding", in which the phobic plunges into the situations he dreads with no means of escape. There are no elements of flooding in this programme, which is based on keeping you well within your controllable anxiety levels throughout.

   However, a key part of the programme involves learning to control your anxiety and it would be wrong of me to suggest that you can recover without experiencing some anxiety. The level of anxiety, however, is always within your personal capacity and at no time will you be overwhelmed.

   Consequently, you must commit to accepting a tolerable level of anxiety as you learn to master and eliminate fear.

4. You must not make the excuse that your phobias are so long-standing and deeply entrenched that they cannot be overcome. This is simply not true. Your body is currently responding to dysfunctional thoughts you have got used to. In the same way you can get used

to helpful thoughts. Your symptoms, distressing as they are, are only superficial. You may well have constructed a whole lifestyle around your difficulties. This too, you must dismantle.

Consequently, you must commit to changing those aspects of your life that are the result of your condition.

5. At the moment you may feel so deeply depressed and exhausted by your phobia that merely thinking about fighting it, causes you distress. For phobics who have endured years of misery the future frequently looks bleak. It is impossible to imagine that you will ever have a better life. If you feel this way then I urge you to at least try it. Give it one month – just four weeks. In that time you will begin to feel better and as you notice the improvements your motivation will blossom.

Consequently, regardless of how bad you feel, you must commit to working at this programme for one month. You can then make an honest assessment of the benefits.

You may accept that the strategies in this book may help others but still insist that they are no use to you. You may have tried several approaches, none of which has worked. So why should you try yet another?

CHOOSE LIFE

You may have tried other approaches, a bit of this and a bit of that, without any success. But what this book offers a structured and detailed programme, which employs a range of strategies to attack all facets of agoraphobia simultaneously and systematically undermine the condition.

However, this is not an instant cure. No single part of this strategy will make a dramatic change. What they will do is make a gradual, almost imperceptible change that will eventually lead to complete recovery, provided you supply the secret ingredient.

The secret ingredient is persistence. You must be dogged, determined and
 persistent. You must never give up. For so long as you accept your condition you are condemning yourself to a life sentence.

If you do not at the present have the motivation to make a start then the only way to get it is by taking positive action to undermine your phobias now. This will give you the motivation. Making the first step will give you confidence and the more you do the more your confidence and motivation will grow and the better you will feel. If you do not make a start nothing will happen and nothing will change.

ESCAPE!

Is that what you want?

ACTION POINTS

1. Complete the following questionnaire.

What would you like to do which your condition now prevents you from doing?

Write them down under the following headings.
Holidays:

....

(Find at least one colour picture of each place you list, cut it out and use it to mark this page.)
Social   Life

....

Employment

....

Hobbies

....

Entertainment

....

Trips   out   (day   trips)

....

Shopping

....

Visiting   friends   and   family

....

2. When you have read through to the end of the book, return to this page. Read the following contract. Within seven days of completing the book you should sign and date

ESCAPE!

it. That date is your first day on the programme.

I .... (full name) agree to put aside any reservations and to embark on the programme fully committed and determined to give of my best. In doing so I commit myself to the following.

i) To begin today on the first of the in vivo exercises, the lowest level of one of my hierarchies;
ii) To continue working through these hierarchies for at least two sessions every week until I have mastered all levels;
iii) To make time every day to work on reducing my general level of anxiety;
iv) To change those aspects of my life which presently reinforce my condition;
v) To tolerate the unavoidable but manageable level of anxiety without which recovery is impossible;
vi) To work through negative feelings and not allow them to deflect me from recovery.

Signed   ....
Date............................

Simply by making this commitment you are starting to change your attitude to your condition and to yourself. You are no longer a helpless victim. Tackling your fears is the major way to restore your confidence.

There are, however, many more things you can do to restore your battered self-esteem. This is the subject of the next chapter.

CHAPTER 4

SELF-ESTEEM

- ➢ Loss of confidence
- ➢ Getting started
- ➢ Telling others
- ➢ What we believe
- ➢ Strategies for restoring self-esteem
- ➢ Dealing with guilt
- ➢ Self-talk
- ➢ Action Point
- ➢ Worry
- ➢ Breaking the chain
- ➢ Shifting the focus
- ➢ Accentuate the positive
- ➢ Action Point
- ➢ Planning
- ➢ Action Point
- ➢ Coming off tranquillisers
- ➢ Goals
- ➢ Action Point
- ➢ Making Excuses

CONFIDENCE IS THE FIRST CASUALTY OF AGORAPHOBIA

Nothing undermines you like not being able to do what everyone else does without a thought. Being dependent on family and friends can rob you of all self-reliance. This loss of confidence filters into every facet of life, undermining your work, relationships and social life.

This is not of the type of ego bruising people suffer all the time, when they fail in a job application or go through the breakdown of a relationship. Such things are unpleasant and may even lead us to reappraise certain aspects of our lives.

But what the agoraphobic undergoes is a profound crisis in which he feels he has lost control of his life. His emotions and thoughts are in turmoil and he feels at the mercy of forces he can neither understand nor influence.

Healthy self-esteem is essential if you are to live a full and rewarding life. Furthermore, it is vital if you are going to make and sustain a commitment to recovery.

One of the things that makes agoraphobia so damaging to a confidence is the ignorance that surrounds the condition. This ignorance is a fertile soil for fears and pessimistic thoughts.

Nor is this ignorance confined to lay people. A leading authority on the treatment of agoraphobia, Claire Weekes, recounts what happened at a clinical psychology conference in the mid nineteen-eighties. It was necessary for her to explain to a group of psychiatric health professionals what panic attacks are and her explanation was met with scepticism by a few senior psychiatrists who doubted that such attacks really happened.

So how do you muster the confidence you need to tackle agoraphobia when one of its effects is a lack of confidence? How do you break out of this most cruel of vicious circles?

GETTING STARTED

The first step to recovery is accepting that you are suffering from agoraphobia. Lots of people, rather than accept the truth, spend a great deal of time and money seeking an alternative explanation. Why?

Because there is still a stigma attached to certain types of illness. If people cannot understand something – such as agoraphobia – they react with fear. The only way to remove this fear is to help them to understand. You remove your own fear by understanding what agoraphobia is and, just as importantly, what it is not. Then you accept it. You help those close to you to overcome their fear by explaining it to them. There is no alternative.

ACTIVITY 1

First you must recognise your symptoms for what they are and accept them as part of the condition. In reading up to this point you have given some thought to your symptoms. This is important because many of them may be so long established that you hardly think of them as symptoms. Now make a list of them. After each one say to yourself, "This is a symptom of my condition. It is perfectly normal for someone with my condition to feel this way. It does not mean I am going mad nor does it mean that I will always feel this way. These symptoms will disappear as I work towards recovery. For the moment, however, I accept them and realise there is no point in railing against them or blaming myself for them."

TELLING OTHERS

A major step in accepting your condition is telling others. Agoraphobics waste so much time and energy concealing their condition instead of directing their efforts towards recovery. Don't make excuses for your avoidance any more – tell the truth.

You will be amazed at the immediate sense of relief this brings. You have removed all the fear of being found out which fuels your anxiety and increases your sense of isolation.

By breaking down your feeling of isolation you are making it possible for friends and relations to help you through recovery. Telling others also has a further major advantage.

By keeping your fears to yourself you are certainly exaggerating their importance. In sharing them with others you are subjecting them to a reality check that is important if you are to put them in perspective.

In preparing to tell others about your condition it may help to remember that doctors in some countries think of agoraphobia as a physical condition and call it 'primary hyperventilation syndrome'. In other words, they regard it as the result of a physical malfunctioning just like diabetes or heart palpitations. Thinking of it this way helps some people to realise that there is no reason why they should be ashamed of their condition.

Yet the prospect of telling people may be daunting. It requires courage especially if you have gone to great lengths to conceal your condition. But you may be pleasantly surprised. Most people may know little or nothing about agoraphobia but what they lack in knowledge may be more than made up for in compassion. Many people react by immediately revealing their own fears. For me telling the truth about my condition was one of the most uplifting experiences of my life. The understanding and generosity with which they responded made me ashamed of my reticence.

So what do you tell people?

It's important to give them the whole picture otherwise they may misunderstand. How you put it, is of course, dependent on your assessment of

ESCAPE!

what is appropriate. It is however important that you make certain points clear.

Say that you have difficulty with a type of anxiety called agoraphobia. Make it clear that this is not a mental illness but a form of intense worry that leads to panic attacks. Sometimes they occur out of the blue but certain situations, such as confined spaces, crowds, travelling on motorways and being away from home, trigger them and this is why you avoid these situations. Explain that panics are very unpleasant and that you are concerned about how people might react to seeing you having an attack.

Tell people that you are currently working through a programme to overcome these difficulties and that you are improving. However, make it clear that panic attacks remain a problem and there are occasions when you may have to leave the room. Explain that it helps you a great deal to know that people understand the reasons for this and do not think your behaviour odd.

If the person you are telling expresses understanding please do not miss the opportunity to thank him and reiterate that it helps a lot to know that he understands.

WHAT WE BELIEVE

There is no doubt that it helps to know that people do not think ill of us because of our condition. But it is far more important that we do not think ill of ourselves because of it.

To a large extent we are what we believe we are. A good self-image allows us to concentrate on our achievements and develop a positive approach to our problems. It is vital to make a conscious effort to cultivate those habits that foster a strong self-image.

This is why you must always think of yourself in positive terms. Do not put yourself down or criticise yourself because of your condition. Do not blame yourself for something that is beyond your control.

Think positively about your condition. Do not define yourself in terms agoraphobia. Look on it as a temporary phase you are working through. There was a time when you were not agoraphobic and that time will come again if you tackle the problem in a systematic way.

ESCAPE!

STRATEGIES FOR RESTORING SELF-ESTEEM

The most important thing you can do to restore your self-esteem is to make up your mind to get better and promise yourself that you will not give up before you have achieved your goal. It is impossible to put too much emphasis on this point.

Once you have made this decision your spirits immediately soar. By committing yourself to a programme of recovery you are taking control of your life and refusing to remain a victim of your condition. You are recognising for perhaps the first time that your condition is not a life sentence and that you are capable of bringing about your own recovery.

One of the most invidious effects of agoraphobia is that it removes the enjoyment from almost everything you try to do. Instead of a warm glow of satisfaction pervading the things you once loved – spending times with friends, watching films, going out for meals – a grey pall hangs over everything. This tendency for things to lose their sparkle is one of many distressing symptoms and if it not checked it can pervade all facets of your life.

HOW DO I COUNTER IT?

Here as with so many other aspects of the condition it is important to remind yourself that this is not a permanent state. You should not give up the things you used to enjoy but instead make a conscious effort to appreciate them. Focus your attention on those things you still enjoy.

For instance, if you go out for a meal and, looking back on it, feel that you did not really enjoy the evening, give the matter a little more thought. Was there nothing about it you enjoyed? The food, a joke someone told, the ambience of the restaurant, the break from routine? Was there not some stage during the course of the evening when you forgot your worries and actually felt relaxed? Even if this lasted for only a short time it is something positive you got out of the evening. In order to fully appreciate it you should write it down.

You should also plan social events or treats and make sure they actually happen. Aim for at least one major treat every week and at least one minor treat every day.

DEALING WITH GUILT

Few things are as corrosive as guilt. It is capable of destroying anyone's self-esteem but agoraphobics are particularly prone to its damaging effects. Many feel guilty because of the restrictions their condition has imposed on their family, perhaps depriving them of holidays or limiting their social lives. Many agoraphobics' partners voluntarily restrict their lives, sometimes even giving up work.

Sometimes agoraphobics feel guilty because they think their condition has made them a disappointment to their family. Perhaps they feel they have not taken a full part in the upbringing of their children. There is in fact no aspect of their condition – real or imaginary – about which agoraphobics cannot feel guilty.

The problem with this type of guilt is that it undermines self-esteem and adds to anxiety. This is why you must address it.

The first step is to accept your guilt. It is important not to deny it but to acknowledge it.

Next search out its cause. Do you feel guilty because of something you have done or not done that affects only you? Or do you blame yourself because of the way you have acted towards others?

Analyse your guilt feelings by filling in the boxes below. Do this for each of the things you feel guilty about.

ACTION POINTS

1. Precisely what did you do or say?
2. When did you do this?
3. Why did you do it? Be totally honest. When you performed this action did you know its consequences or were they unforeseen?
4. What effects did this action have on you or others? Do not surmise or speculate – confine yourself to those consequences of which you are sure.
5. Is there any way in which you can make amends for the harm you caused? Write down the specific ways you might do this: by paying for the damage you caused, by undoing it or simply by apologising.
6. How would you feel about another person who did exactly what you did? Would you be able to understand his actions and forgive him? If so why should you not forgive yourself?
7. Write down what you have learnt from this incident that will affect your behaviour in future. This is something you have gained from the experience. It is important that you amend your behaviour accordingly.
8. Now make a conscious decision to forgive yourself. It is wrong to say, 'I can't forgive myself no matter how I try.' Forgiveness is a matter of will. You must decide that you

are going to forgive yourself and then do it. Fill in section 7 of the form.

9. Commit yourself to reading this page once every day for the next month. Thereafter you should reread this section on the first day of every month for as long as you feel it is necessary. Guilt will not disappear immediately. It may take a long time but you have made a start.

SELF-TALK

Self-talk is what got you into this mess in the first place.

You talked yourself into thinking that terrible things would happen if you got on a bus, went into a crowded shop or drove on the motorway. All these harmless things frighten you because you talked yourself into believing they are dangerous.

Over and over again, you told yourself that these things were threatening. You told yourself that you could not cope with them. You predicted that confronting them would be a catastrophe. You convinced yourself that there was nothing you could do to counter these fears and you made yourself a helpless victim. You relived your panics and convinced yourself that even worse would happen in the future. You created a prison of your own thoughts. Negative thinking becomes automatic and negative thoughts are self-fulfilling.

They are the filter through which you view the world and they determine your reaction to the world.

As well as undermining your confidence, this type of inner monologue destroys your peace of mind and creates a negative and depressing outlook that leaches all the colour and vitality from life.

It's necessary to break out of this by consciously and systematically confronting your negative thoughts. Unless you do this they will continue to reign supreme and colour your life.

Challenging and changing negative thinking, as I explained in Chapter 3, is called cognitive therapy. As a treatment for severe and mild depression clinical trials have proved it is as effective as antidepressant drug therapy. Its great advantage is that it is so practical and common sense – so much so that it seems too simple and too obvious to work. Yet the most rigorous scientific scrutiny has shown that it does work and that patients who have undertaken this mood training improve their confidence and self-esteem.

Cognitive therapy is based on the principle that what you think determines the way you feel. When you are down you have a negative view of the world – a distorted picture – that everything is black and hopeless. Soon you come to believe that this is really the case.

ESCAPE!

There are three stages to changing your negative and destructive thoughts.

First, you have to spot these negative thoughts.

You may well ask how this is possible as there are so many negative thoughts zapping round your head. However, these grim images, doom-laden thoughts and forebodings, are more than negative thoughts – they are what psychiatrists call cognitive distortions. In other words they are more than separate and discrete ideas. They are a set of incorrect and damaging ideas that run right through your way of looking at the world – each a different way of misinterpreting the world that keeps you scared.

Fortunately they fall into certain categories.

All-or-Nothing thinking or perfectionism leads you to conclude that anything that is not absolutely ideal is a total disaster. If it's not exquisite it's totally worthless. This is black and white thinking in the extreme.

The problem with this is that you are setting yourself up for constant disappointment because reality rarely measures up to perfection. This type of thinking leads you to believe that because you feel slightly anxious when people come round to dinner the whole evening is a disaster.

Overgeneralization is the sort of thinking that leads you to believe that because something went wrong once it is always going to go wrong. Rejected by one girl you conclude you are never going to get a date.

For the agoraphobic this type of thinking causes him to believe that because he currently finds it difficult to travel on the motorway this will always be the case. He is blocking out the fact that it is quite possible to overcome this fear.

Mental filter is a way of looking at life through dark glasses that cut out all the sunshine. This sort of thinking causes you to pick out a negative point about a situation and conclude that everything in the situation is negative. Someone who gets two questions wrong out of 100 in an exam and then dwells on this to exclusion of all he got right is the victim of this thinking. The agoraphobic who has a problem with buses and yet travels ten stops may find that his mental filter cuts out all the positive aspects of the experience and results in him remembering only the first few minutes of the journey during which he felt extremely anxious. The fact that he coped with this anxiety and successfully completed the journey is totally forgotten.

Disqualifying the positive is a way of convincing yourself that nothing good can ever happen to you. The agoraphobic, who has a wonderful day and feels quite relaxed for the first time in a long time, does not tell himself that this is a sign that his condition is improving. Instead he convinces himself that today does not count – because today he was on holiday, because today was a particularly sunny, because today he has no worries. The list is infinite.

Agoraphobics love jumping to conclusions – they love to explain things in the most depressing way. One way in which they do this is by mind reading. For instance, when he feels particularly tense the agoraphobic will tell himself that people are looking at him and wondering what is wrong with him.   In fact, he has no way of knowing what people are thinking. It is almost certain that they are totally unaware of his anxiety and are preoccupied with their own thoughts. Even if someone were conscious of his distress they would probably assume there was a perfectly good reason for it, such as a bout of indigestion.

Agoraphobics also go in for fortune telling. During a panic attack they invariably tell themselves that they are going to die or pass out – even though this has never happened. They like to tell themselves that they are never going to get better and that their condition is going to deteriorate.

Agoraphobics have a tendency to look at aspects of their lives through a telescope. They turn every glitch into a catastrophe. When they are looking at their faults and failings, they use the telescope to magnify them. They tell themselves that a single setback, such as a panic attack, is proof that their situation is hopeless and that will never improve.

When it comes to looking at their achievements and progress towards recovery, however, they look down the other end of the telescope. So, when an agoraphobic makes a breakthrough by entering a phobic situation for the first time in years, instead of celebrating it as a breakthrough he tells himself that it doesn't mean anything.

Emotional reasoning is another stick the agoraphobic uses to beat himself. What happens here is that he assumes that his feelings are proof that something is true. So, because he feels at low ebb and cannot imagine a time when he will be well, he takes this as proof that his condition is hopeless.

Another trick agoraphobics use to keep themselves trapped in their condition involves the use of 'should statements,' such as 'I should be able to do this,' 'I should have the willpower to conquer my fears', 'I should snap out of this.'

Very often the agoraphobic tries to use these statements to motivate himself. He feels that these 'should statements' are the only means by which he can get himself to do things. The result is, however, the opposite. Such statements, with their burden of moral weight, result in him feeling pressured, resentful and dispirited. Falling short of these targets makes him feel shame, self-loathing and guilt.

Agoraphobics love labelling and mislabelling, because this enables them to write themselves off with a single sweeping insult. So agoraphobics like to say things like, 'I'm a loser,' 'I'm no good,' and 'I'm a total waste of space.'

Finally, as if they did not have enough problems of their own, agoraphobics like to blame themselves for things that are not their own fault. They often blame themselves for their condition by saying things like, 'If I wasn't such a coward I wouldn't have this condition,' and 'No one else has these problems.' This way of looking at things gives rise to guilt.

Do not misunderstand. Agoraphobics do not choose to think this way. Until it is pointed out to them, they are not aware of this negative, self-defeating mindset which has crept up on them and locked them into a circle of self-fulfilling prophesies of doom.

Nevertheless, these cognitive distortions are extremely damaging and when combined with low self-esteem they prevent the agoraphobic from embarking on a programme of recovery. So how do you eliminate them?

There are five stages to countering these damaging thoughts.

1. Learn to recognise this distorted thinking. Read and reread the section above until you are so familiar with the forms of cognitive distortion that you can instantly recognise them in your own thinking.
2. Stop your automatic inner monologue from being automatic. Monitor what you are saying to yourself and identify each form of cognitive distortion as it appears.
3. Talk back to your inner critic: train yourself to recognise and write down the self-critical thoughts as they go through your mind. Use the sheets in the appendix for this purpose. This is extremely valuable because it stops the thoughts from buzzing around in your head unchallenged. Now you are pinning them down and challenging them.
4. Practise talking back to them to develop a more realistic self-evaluation system. What you write in the response column must be realistic and convincing. Doing them in your head is no good on its own – writing them down helps you to achieve far more objectivity than if you do it in your head.
5. To refute negative thoughts about yourself you must first accept that you are not a stagnant entity, set in stone for

all time. We are all changing all the time – we are in state of flux. Even our faults are not unalterable – we can learn from our mistakes and improve for the better. Because you feel bad about yourself this does not mean you are a worthless person. It means that you feel bad about yourself because you have negative thoughts which are unrealistic and which are subject to change.

ACTION POINT

Turn to the Cognitive Distortion Sheet in the Appendix. Before you write on it make a number of copies.

Set aside a few minutes now to address one negative thought you have had today. For the next three weeks do the same each day. Try to deal with a different type of negative thinking for each of the first seven days.

Joseph O'Neill

WORRY

The agoraphobic exists in a permanent state of tension, verging on panic. This free-floating anxiety seems to be part of the air he breathes. Many situations make this worse. There are, of course, the phobic situations that you go to so much trouble to avoid. But unfortunately these are not the only causes of powerful anxiety feelings.

All those situations that provoke anxiety in people who are not suffering from a phobia take an even greater toll on the agoraphobic. A visit to the dentist, conflict with a colleague, family or financial problems pose enormous difficulties.

Most of the time, he may be able to control this to the extent that he can keep panic at bay. But the tension is something he cannot keep at bay.

This tension and stress results in a number of symptoms that can be very worrying. This worry in turn adds to the tension. The first step in removing this worry is to explain the cause of the symptoms.

Many of these symptoms are physical.

Agoraphobics frequently feel queasy and often suffer from stomach cramps. The extra adrenaline sloshing round your system when you are in a state of anxiety has the effect of producing surplus acid in the stomach. This produces a feeling of indigestion or sickness. It may also result in stomach cramps. This too is the result of the adrenaline causing painful spasms in the muscles of the bowel.

Diarrhoea, another condition suffered by agoraphobics, is often the result of the direct action of adrenaline on the bowel.

Tremors in the hands and legs are the result of muscle tension, the result of stress.

One of the most worrying consequences of stress is palpitations. We notice a gap between heartbeats. This too is the result of surplus adrenaline that makes your heart first put in the extra beat and later skip a beat. It is completely harmless.

Headaches are often the result of knotted neck muscles caused by tension. Press the muscles with your thumb. If you feel a resistance in the muscle and discomfort after you have removed the pressure this is a sign that it is caused by tension. This type of muscle tension is also the result of too much adrenaline in the blood stream or of over-breathing. The same type of tightness in the throat muscles can make it uncomfortable to swallow.

Similarly, tension and muscle pains in the shoulders are the body's way of reacting to anxiety. In the same way dizziness and shortness of breath may be the result of tightness in the muscles joining the ribs together.

A related effect is extreme tiredness, which is often the result of tension in the muscles. This is why agoraphobics do not feel refreshed when they wake in the morning. The habit of tensing muscles has become habitual and happens even when they are asleep.

Knowing the cause of these physical symptoms helps to remove the fear that naturally arises when you cannot find an explanation for them. Just as important, once you have identified the cause you can do something about tackling them. Chapters 6, 7 and 8 deal with ways to eliminate all the physical effects of anxiety so that you once more feel healthy and well. Relaxation almost immediately alleviates many of these symptoms and removes others. The result is a more tranquil frame of mind.

This is another area in which you immediately feel better as soon as you start to tackle your problems. If, however, you have any concerns about your health contact your doctor.

ESCAPE!

WORRY

Here I am not talking about cognitive distortion. That is dealt with above. What I am concerned with here is obsessive worry and gloominess that pervades your whole outlook. This results in preoccupation with problems that are often trivial. Yet you turn them over and over in your mind, magnifying them and destroying your peace of mind.

Mystics know that we all gravitate towards those things that fill our thoughts. Our minds attract what we think about. Bright, optimistic and positive people seem to enjoy untroubled lives. The grim and aggrieved attract misfortune.

Pervasive worry drains your energy and saps your will. It often springs from a sense of inferiority, low self-esteem and inadequacy. Habit has such great power over you that you are probably convinced that it is impossible to change.

This is especially so when these thoughts seem to take on a momentum of their own. It's as if our thinking is trapped in a destructive look and no matter how we try we cannot escape it. This compulsive worry can be so distressing that it prevents you from eating, sleeping or gaining any peace of mind.

Chapters 6, 7 and 8 deal with the long-term solutions to this problem. In the meantime, however, there are a number of strategies for gaining immediate relief.

BREAKING THE CHAIN

Sometimes simply telling yourself to stop, either by shouting, "Stop!" or by saying it to yourself in a firm and confident inner voice, can break the train of thought. Practise will quickly improve your ability to do this.

Work through the following the procedure every day until you can control your obsessive worrying.

- ✓ Think of a situation is which you normally experience negative thoughts. Perhaps you have these thoughts on a Sunday evening as you think about going to work on a Monday morning. Or it could be the prospect of travelling on public transport that fills you with worry.
- ✓ Bring to mind those negative thoughts. Make a conscious effort to experience the sensations you have in this situation.
- ✓ Shout 'Stop!' and at the same time snap your fingers or clap your hands.
- ✓ Practice this several times until you find it breaks the train of negative thoughts.
- ✓ When you next have a negative thought, shout 'Stop!' Continue with this every time you have

ESCAPE!

these destructive thoughts and feelings until you are able to disrupt them.

✓ The next time you start worrying, say 'Stop' in your normal speaking voice. Again, continue with this until it is effective.

✓ Thereafter, simply disrupt the chain of negative thoughts by saying 'Stop' in your mind, with your internal voice.

✓ You can reinforce this with an elastic band, which you wear on your arm or wrist. When you say 'Stop' snap the band against your skin.

✓ Thereafter use this strategy to disrupt the chain of worry as soon as you are aware of them.

SHIFTING THE FOCUS

Many people find vigorous physical activity – jogging, cycling, using a cross-trainer or playing squash -- extremely helpful. These things work so well because they shift your attention from negative thoughts to the things your body is doing. Perhaps this is why many people find that household chores or tidying and sorting tasks are also helpful.

Of course, there are many occasions when this is not possible and when alternatives such as a brisk walk or a bout of abdominal breathing may be more practical.

If you are a reader then few things are more engrossing than an enjoyable book.

I find that alternative nostril breathing never fails. Part of the reason is that it requires a level of concentration to count the breaths, which is incompatible with obsessive worry.

Progressive relaxation and any of the other relaxation methods outlined in this book will also have the same beneficial effect.

As well as these emergency measures, it is important to challenge the drip, drip, drip of poison that is obsessive worry. Tackling it on an emotional level can be as effective as tackling negative self-talk in a logical way.

ESCAPE!

When a negative thought comes into your head tell yourself that you are not going to allow this automatic, reflex thinking to make you feel bad about yourself. State clearly and emphatically that you are not going to tolerate it and confront it with rational challenges. When you start thinking, ' I'm so fed up today' ask yourself if you want to feel that way. The answer of course is no. So why not remind yourself of something good that has happened to you today? Mentally rehearse the things you have enjoyed today. Write them down and savour them. Do not dismiss anything as too insignificant.

Reminding yourself of the good things in your life is extremely important. 'Count your blessings' is a sound psychology. By enumerating your blessings and making yourself aware of them you are taking a positive step towards improving your frame of mind.

Each night as you lie in bed about to fall asleep, go over the good things that have happened to you during the day. At first you may find this difficult as you are so used to focusing on problems and difficulties. Try to bring to mind ten good things from the day. Think about the people you have met during the day and bring to mind the ways in which they enrich your life – the love you get from a devoted partner, the joy of your children, the support of colleagues, the boost from a stranger's smile. Relive each of these incidents.

ACCENTUATING THE POSITIVE

To someone who is an habitual pessimist, whose default mode is doggedly negative, the idea that repeating positive statements can modify your outlook seems puerile, the worst type of psycho-drivel. If you are this sort of person you are likely to feel very uncomfortable with this idea and to reject it as a tone-deaf introvert might shudder at the prospect of karaoke.

This was exactly my reaction.

Nevertheless I decided to give it a go, confident that it would soon prove to be a load of rubbish. I started like the reluctant golfer, playing only to humour the boss, secretly despising golf-bores. Soon I was practising my swing.

Suspend your scepticism for just one week. Apply this strategy in a totally uncritical way and see if it makes a difference. My guess is that you will be amazed by the effect it has on your frame of mind.

First, you will begin to take a detached and critical view of what you are thinking. Previously you accepted your thoughts as a part of your personality, something you were stuck with. Now you will see that you have the power to decide what you tell yourself. Never again will your inner voice be able to drag you down unopposed.

ESCAPE!

Secondly, you will find that the positive statements you keep repeating make you feel better. Even if you can muster no conviction as you repeat them, keep on repeating them. They will do their work despite your scepticism.

Now try the following.

- Study the positive statements of affirmation below. Feel free to modify or add to them to make them more specific to your unique qualities and strengths.
- Pick the ten statements you find most powerful.
- Write each one on a piece of card, such as an index card, in a small notebook you can carry around with you or as memos on a mobile phone.
- At least three times a day read through them slowly. Consider each one for a few seconds, allowing yourself to feel how true it is.
- When you have a spare five minutes during the day, read through your list and remind yourself of why they are true.
- As soon as a piece of negative self-talk comes into your head, immediately challenge it in the way discussed above. Then look through your list and find the most appropriate counter statement. Repeat it several times.
- You will soon find that you know by heart the counter statements you use most often. This means they are becoming part of your mental furniture. They have now become a permanent

challenge to your negative thoughts. You are creating an alternative outlook and destructive attitudes no longer have the free run of your mind.

- Choose your tens statements from the following list:
- I have many qualities.
- I am made in the image and likeness of God and have His unconditional love.
- I am learning to overcome my fears.
- I am getting stronger, fitter and healthier every day.
- I feel good about the future. Things are improving.
- I am learning to take control of my life and overcome my difficulties.
- I have many people who love and support me.
- I don't have to be perfect to deserve my own respect and the love of others.
- I have confidence in my worth and my ability.
- I am proud of many things in my life.
- I'm looking forward with confidence to the challenges I have set myself.
- I have the right to spend time on getting better. I owe it to myself.
- I am learning to attend to my needs.
- I am feeling more confident every day.
- Every day, in every way, I am getting better and better.
- I am learning not to worry.
- I no longer put myself down.

ESCAPE!

- I am enjoying the good things that are happening to me.
- I am setting and achieving goals every day.
- I am the master of my own destiny. Nothing can stop me.

Getting rid of negative thoughts works best when it is combined with changing behaviour. This is why the activities described in Chapters 6, 7, 8 and 9 are so important.

There is no better start to the day than Coue's famous mantra: Every day, in every way, I am getting better and better. Repeat this twenty times upon waking.

Always speak in positive terms. Speak of 'Doing this' not 'Do not do this.' Always think in terms of what you do want, not in terms of what you want to avoid. Dwell on what you want in a positive way.

ACTION PLAN

Read the list of statements above. If you can write statements that seem more powerful or more relevant to you, do so. Now choose the best ten. Put them into a notebook or some other means which allows you to carry them about with you. Refer to them during the course of the day.

PLANNING

Planning is the key to reducing stress. It introduces regularity and structure to our lives and removes a great deal of the uncertainty that agoraphobics find unsettling. It also gives us a degree of control, which enhances our self-esteem.

Planning helps to achieve a balanced life. Without it many people allow work to monopolise their time to the neglect of family, friends, hobbies and social life. Many things we intend to do will forever remain good intentions unless we schedule them.

What is important in life depends very much on your priorities. An important first step is working out these priorities.

Ask yourself what really matters to you. What interests should you develop in order to enrich your life? Use the questionnaire in the Appendix to help you work out your priorities.

A balanced and healthy life should be a regular one. Refreshing sleep is very important and you are most likely to get it if you keep regular hours. Exercise is a great boon to recovery and you should try to build it into your routine so that you have at least four twenty-minute sessions each week. Taking proper breaks for meals is also

ESCAPE!

important. You will feel better and it will increase your concentration and productivity.

You may protest that this is impossible because you do not have the time. It is possible that this is true but what is more likely is that you are taking on tasks, which you could delegate to others. Spend a few moments running through the tasks you perform at work and at home. Jot down ways in which it might be possible for you to lighten the load to make room in your life for other things.

Our family can be among our greatest joys. Make time for them and try to listen when they speak. One of the pitfalls of agoraphobia is becoming self-obsessed. If we find ourselves so absorbing that we have no interest in others we can hardly expect people to have any interest in us.

It is important to maintain and develop a network of friends. This requires time and effort. We lose most friends not because of any falling out but because we are careless about maintaining contact.

Make time for hobbies and leisure activities. Give yourself treats and rewards for positive actions and rewards. Listen carefully to those around you.

Enjoyment is the best cure for stress. Have pockets of delight built into every day – times when you listen to music, read, make model aeroplanes or whatever gives you pleasure.

ACTION POINT

Make a list of the five most important things in your life, the people, relationships or activities that are most important to you. Rank them in order of importance.

Next to each one jot down the average number of hours you devote to each in an average week. It is important that you are totally honest.

If this exercise suggests a mismatch between what you value and how you spend your time, find three ways to redress this imbalance. Write them down.

When you have read Chapters 6 to 9 you will want to incorporate into your routine many of the procedures for overcoming your condition. You can address this later but for now use your questionnaire to plan your days so that you devote time to the things that are important to you.

ESCAPE!

COMING OFF TRANQUILLIZERS

The hazards of long term use of tranquillisers, particularly benzodiazepines, are well documented. The promotion and prescription of these drugs has been the subject of protracted litigation.

One of the major difficulties of long-term tranquilliser use is its effect on self-esteem. There is no doubt that it is extremely damaging to self-confidence.

There are, however, many other good reasons to withdraw.

Tranquillisers often have side effects – dizziness, drowsiness, headaches, poor co-ordination. These can be as unpleasant as the symptoms the tranquillisers were prescribed to avoid.

Besides, long-tern use is often a way of avoiding the underlying problem for which they were first prescribed. They damp down your fears. But they also dull the emotions and make it less likely you will confront the underlying problem.

Fortunately there is an alternative to tranquillisers. You can learn to control your anxiety without them.

Long-term users, however, usually develop some degree of dependence and withdrawal invariably has some unpleasant effects. These may include:

- Palpitations
- Sleeplessness
- Aches and pains
- Restlessness
- Headaches
- Over-sensitivity to noise, light and touch
- Pins and needles
- Loss of appetite
- Trembling
- Sweating
- Feelings of sickness
- Increase in anxiety
- Loss of confidence
- Poor concentration and memory
- Tension
- Feelings of unreality

It is important to remember, not everyone has these symptoms and no one will have all of them. You can greatly reduce the number and intensity of symptoms by gradual withdrawal. No one recommends cold turkey.

Remember that despite what you might feel these symptoms are not the return of your original anxiety. They are temporary symptoms and will disappear when your body adjusts to the changes.

ESCAPE!

Before starting withdrawal discuss the matter with your doctor. Explain your concerns and ask for his advice. Obviously, as he is the health professional who knows your circumstances, you should be guided by him.

If you decide to go ahead with withdrawal ask for your doctor's support. You may welcome the experience of a 'Tranquilliser Withdrawal Support Group.' (See Appendix for details.)

Withdrawal is not easy. You will almost certainly encounter difficulties. When they arise you should consider the following strategies for making the task manageable:

✓ Do not tell yourself that you are giving up tranquillisers forever. Tell yourself that you are managing without them just for today. If this seems too difficult, think in terms of the next hour or thirty minutes.

✓ You need to remind yourself of the reason why you are giving up tranquillisers. Use the strategies explained in the section of Chapter 8 on giving up cigarettes.

✓ You may well find that by telling others what you are doing you enlist their help. You may use your helper.

✓ Keep busy. By planning to fully occupy your time you make it easier to get through the day. Again, the things you used to help with cigarette withdrawal also apply.

✓ Keep a record. Note all the positive effects of giving up and describe in detail the good days.

These can provide you with a real source of strength when you are going through difficult times.

✓ Use all the anxiety reduction and management strategies I explain. Practise will improve your mastery of these skills and reduce your need for tranquillisers.

ESCAPE!

GOALS

Nothing enhances self-esteem like achievement. When you set yourself a goal – no matter how small it is – and achieve it, you get a sense of achievement. Goals, targets, challenges – call them what you will – are vital for giving our lives a sense of purpose. At least one major piece of research into the differences between happy and unhappy people has come to the conclusion that setting and achieving goals is the way to contentment. It does not much matter what they are – it is the process of achieving them that makes us happy.

For a phobic confronting his difficulties, entering the situations you previously avoided is a major accomplishment. The more you do it the more your self-esteem flourishes. What will certainly give you a major boost is mastering strategies for handling the fears that inevitably arise. Persisting with a graded programme of desensitisation is the single most important thing you can do to raise your self-esteem and develop a positive self-image.

Lots of people suffering from agoraphobia stagnate physically, socially and emotionally. Their development is suspended. As your world gets narrower and narrower and you turn in on yourself and as your appetite for activities is dulled, you lose your capacity for enjoyment. You lose sight of those things that add variety and texture to life and close the door to joy and contentment. In effect, you give up trying to enjoy yourself and settle instead for a bland, panic-free existence.

You justify this by making excuses – too ill, the wrong time, when I feel better. It is not only agoraphobics who do this. But a pronounced tendency towards procrastination is part of the condition, the tendency to suspend our lives until things get better. As I have said many times, things will not get better on their own without you taking a hand in changing your situation. You have to accept responsibility for your own life and strive to change it in ways that fit in with your aims.

As you start to tackle your problems you will become more confident. You will want to do more with your life and become more ambitious. It is as if you have released the brake you put on your aspirations.

Because you have failed to do this in the past, you have lost a sense of your own capacity to influence your life and this in turn leads to a feeling of depression and impotence.

It needn't be like that. Setting goals and striving for them is the surest ways of improving your sense of well being and strengthening your resolve to recover.

ESCAPE!

As in so many of the areas this book deals with, changing this situation for the better will not happen merely by thinking about it. It will only happen by following through a clear strategy. The first step is to define your goals.

Make a list of your goals. There are numerous headings under which you can examine your aspirations. Here are some you might use:

- ✓ Health and fitness
- ✓ State of mind
- ✓ Money
- ✓ Significant other
- ✓ Family
- ✓ Home
- ✓ Friends
- ✓ Work
- ✓ Courses / qualifications
- ✓ Interests and hobbies
- ✓ Travel
- ✓ Spiritual life

Over the next few days, give serious consideration to what you hope to achieve in each of these and any other areas of your life. Use the chart in the Appendix to help you. You can add to it or amend it in any way you choose.

Remember that you get back what you put into any area of your life. The process of striving to enrich your life is as important as the result. Try to do things to the best of your ability and derive pleasure from doing them.

Finding motivation can be difficult. You may feel that you can't be bothered or that it's not worthwhile. You must resist this temptation to do nothing. You get motivation by doing things. Do not wait for the motivation or you will wait forever. By doing something you kick start the momentum of change. It may be a hard grind at first but the more you persist the easier it will get.

Keep moving, keep active. Do not stagnate. Look to the bright new future you are shaping for yourself and let go of the past. Live in the present. Do not mope over the time you have wasted in illness. That is beyond your control whereas the future is entirely at your disposal.

ACTION POINT 2

Complete the chart My Priorities in the Appendix. At this stage what you write is provisional. You will be returning to it again, most importantly when you have completed the book.

ESCAPE!

MAKING EXCUSES

Agoraphobics are the world's best makers of excuses. They are capable of justifying anything no matter how damaging it is.

This is something you are going to have to tackle. These are the sort of things you say to yourself to justify not taking action:

- ✓ I've been ill for too long to recover.' The truth is that the symptoms are superficial. You have become sensitised to certain situations – your fear reaction has developed a hair-trigger response. But it is possible to reverse this process in a few months and your ability to do this is not related to the length you have suffered the illness.
- ✓ 'The panics are too dreadful to face.' The truth is that there are many ways in which you can learn to reduce the intensity of panics and control the symptoms. This book tells you how.
- ✓ 'I don't have the strength or resolve to do it.' The truth is that you will acquire the strength and the resolve if you force yourself to practise. You owe it to yourself. You are going to have to be very strict and rigid about sticking to a timetable of recovery and not accepting any excuses from yourself. Keep on keeping on. Do it

now – do not wait until you feel like it. You will only come to feel like it by doing it. The more you confront your fears the more you will feel like it, the more confident you will become and the better you will feel.

✓ 'It's not worth all the trouble.' The truth is recovery will enrich your life more than you can imagine. It will strengthen you and arouse your interest in the world in a way you cannot now envisage. It is a gradual process and you succeed by doing it – not by spending a lot of time thinking about how you are going to do it.

✓ 'Perhaps the drug companies will produce a drug that cures me. Maybe I'll find a psychiatrist who'll cure me.' There is no panacea, no inspired doctor who can cure you. Only you can cure yourself. It depends entirely on you.

More than anything else, agoraphobics are lukewarm about tackling their condition because they fear confronting panic. This is because they believe that panic cannot be controlled.

In the next chapter I will show you that this is not true. Panics, you will see, are a paper tiger.

CHAPTER 5

Countering Panic

➢ What panic can't do
➢ Coping with panic: strategies to defuse fear:
✓ Acceptance
✓ Positive self-talk
✓ Concentrating on what is happening
✓ Coping statements
✓ Countering physical symptoms
✓ Alternative Nostril Breathing
✓ Distraction
✓ Emergency measures

WHAT PANICS CAN'T DO

No one who has had a panic attack ever forgets it – it is indelibly impressed on your mind as a turning point in your life. It would be stupid to minimise the effect of panic attacks or to play down their horror.

But this does not mean that they cannot be conquered. There are many distressing conditions, which, with the right approach can be overcome. Panic is one of them.

Strategies for dealing with panic are like fire exits – you can never have too many of them. All the techniques I explain have something to recommend them. You can discover which ones suit you best only after practising and trying them all. Time spent mastering these techniques is time well spent.

There are certain things you should remember about panic. These principles apply to all the techniques for aborting panic before it mounts to a fully blown attack.

If, at the start of a panic attack, you were to do absolutely nothing, all the symptoms would subside of their own accord. By its nature panic can last for only a short time. Your body works in such a way that it cannot help but bring panic to an end. The average duration of an attack is less than twenty-five minutes and about one in five attacks lasts for less than five minutes. You may be telling yourself that an attack will never end but the reality is that it must end soon. It is physically impossible for your body to sustain it for more than half an hour. As you will see later, you can take steps to both shorten the duration of an attack and to make it less intense.

Even the most intense panic can do you no serious harm. In all the annals of medical history there is not a single example of anyone dying from a panic attack. Not one. Whatever you are telling yourself, you will not die.

Nor are there any examples of people passing out during a panic attack. Quite the contrary, it is impossible for you to lose consciousness during a panic. You may feel light-headed and think that you are going to collapse but it just doesn't happen.

Some people worry about having a stroke – or what life will be like for them after they've had a stroke. Others worry that their eyesight may be affected. Both fears are totally groundless.

Fear of a stroke or a heart attack arises because many agoraphobics become highly sensitive to palpitations. This is understandable, as palpitations are often the first sign of a panic.

Yet palpitations are nothing more than the body's way of evening out the beats of the heart. They occur after a number of rapid beats. By pausing for the length of a beat the heart compensates for the rapid beats that have preceded it. The normal heartbeat soon reasserts itself.

Another common but entirely groundless fear is that of being paralysed.

Less common but equally distressing is the fear of choking during a panic. This is nothing more than temporary muscle tension in the throat. Many people feel unable to swallow. Again, this is simply the result of the saliva in the mouth and throat drying up in response to anxiety. The solution is to make a conscious effort to relax the muscles that have knotted in your throat.

Perhaps the most alarming sensation during a panic attack is the fear that you are unable to breathe and might suffocate. Like all the other distressing physical symptoms of fear, this is perfectly normal. As your body prepares to take flight, it draws in the extra oxygen your muscles need if they are work at maximum capacity. This is why your breathing speeds up. Your body can sustain this for only a limited time and it slows down and returns to normal.

This makes some people think they are suffocating. It cannot happen. You can prove this to yourself by trying to stop yourself from breathing. Hold your breath. No matter how you try to stop yourself from breathing, you can't do it. Nor can a panic attack.

But for some the most frightening aspect of a panic is not physical. It is the fear of going insane. From the very first attack many people are convinced that they are going mad.

This fear is especially likely to trouble those who suffer from an intense sense of unreality during panic. In some cases panic brings on a powerful feeling of being disembodied, of being outside yourself looking down on what is happening. This is most distressing when accompanied by pins and needles in the face, hands or legs as these add to the sense of unreality.

Though extremely distressing, these feelings of impending insanity are totally groundless. To appreciate this it is necessary to understand something about mental illness.

When a layman describes someone as mad or insane he is thinking of major mental illness, what doctors call psychosis. Psychotics lose contact with reality. Some suffer hallucinations in which they are convinced they hear, see or feel things that are not there. Some lose the capacity to think logically while others imagine they are extremely important or powerful people – they may even believe they are a famous historical figures like Napoleon or Hitler. It is quite common for them to imagine that an organisation or group, bent on their destruction, is persecuting them.

Anxiety conditions are fundamentally different. To distinguish them from mental problems some psychiatrists refer to them as emotional problems. These conditions are known as neuroses. The sufferer is perfectly normal in every way and is fully aware that the things he fears are not in themselves harmful.

Furthermore, panic attacks do not cause or lead to mental illness. They are not a symptom of mental illness. They are something entirely different.

A related fear is that of being thought weird or strange. Many agoraphobics are terrified they will make a fool of themselves during a panic. They fear losing control, shouting and screaming, running about and behaving in a way that makes everyone think they're crazy.

There are two points to make here. Firstly, you are acutely aware of your churning stomach, pounding heart and ragged breathing. But the chances are that no one else will notice. Even if you are sitting next to someone on a bus or train he is probably so wrapped up in his newspaper, the events of the day or his plans for the evening that he is oblivious to your discomfort.

Secondly, people do not lose control during a panic attack. Have you ever found yourself running about shouting during a panic? No. Nor has anyone else. Like most things going through your head when you are in the grip of panic, this particular fear is totally without foundation.

The same applies to other common worries – fear of vomiting, losing control of your bladder or bowels and harming other people. These are groundless fears. You are more likely to win the Lottery jackpot than have any of these things happen to you.

One leading authority on panic and agoraphobia summed up the situation when she said that a panic attack cannot harm the sufferer in any way, either mentally or physically. Keep that firmly in mind.

COPING WITH PANICS

One of the most frightening aspects of panic is the feeling that you can't do anything to control it. Like so many other things the phobic tells himself, this is incorrect. However, this feeling of helplessness, that once a panic has started you are totally at its mercy, is no less distressing because it is untrue.

Once you learn how to defuse panic this helplessness disappears.

Before describing the strategies for defusing panic, I'll explain two general principles that underlie all coping strategies.

First, it is always easier to control anxiety in the early stages. This is why spotting the beginnings of tension is so valuable. If, however, you miss these early signs and find that a panic attack is emerging, then you need to have certain back-up strategies at hand.

Secondly, all the strategies I outline required you to adopt a particular attitude to panic. You must accept what is happening to you.

ESCAPE!

ACCEPTANCE

At first this seems to be asking the impossible. Anyone who has ever had a panic attack knows that every fibre of your being tells you to resist it, to fight against it. Your initial reaction is, 'Oh God, don't let this happen.' This is, however, entirely the wrong reaction.

By resisting, by tensing up, gritting your teeth and clenching your fists, you are fuelling the attack and increasing its ferocity.

In order to reduce the power of the attack and dissipate its force you should confront the panic by accepting that you are having an attack. Instead of tensing your body, let it go completely slack. Scan your body and wherever you sense tension, relax the muscles. Do not be impatient if the attack does not seem to be passing. Instead of allowing restlessness to become another source of agitation, allow time to pass.

Doing the opposite of this – doing what we instinctively want to do – increases stress, sensitisation and prolongs the attack. This is like the situation you find when you have a rash. Every instinct tells you to scratch. How else are you going to get rid of the itch? But scratching also inflames your skin and ultimately prolongs the discomfort.

Acceptance and patient resignation deflates the panic, causing it to collapse. You are wrong-footing your enemy.

In doing this you will learn a vital lesson about panic. It comes in a wave and instead of engulfing you it dissipates itself. It runs its natural course – which is to rise and then fall. It will not rise and rise. This is physically impossible, despite what you keep telling yourself.

By confronting your fear and facing it you realise that you were being bluffed by physical symptoms.

Some psychiatrists believe that this has proved a vital turning point for many patients. From this point on they have made rapid progress. I remember the first time I mastered this technique. I was on a crowded train, standing in the aisle and feeling extremely agitated. As soon as I felt a panic starting, I made a conscious effort to accept it and relax tense muscles. The panic immediately aborted.

ESCAPE!

POSITIVE SELF-TALK

Having adopted an accepting disposition, you are ready to get the maximum benefit from coping strategies.

Write down the steps outlined below in a small notebook, on index cards or a mobile phone's memo so you always have them with you. When you feel an attack coming on, read the instructions in a calm, slow voice. If you are on your own, speak the words aloud.

- ✓ These feelings are the normal bodily reaction to stress. They are totally harmless and cannot damage me in any way.
- ✓ I am not going to fuel the physical symptoms by indulging in unhelpful thoughts. Instead I am going to use one of the strategies I have learnt for replacing these negative thoughts with ones that are more realistic and helpful.
- ✓ I am accepting what is happening. I am allowing it to wash over me while I concentrate on anxiety management strategies.
- ✓ When this has passed I am going to carry on with what I was doing. I will proceed in a calm and relaxed way, knowing that I have had the opportunity to develop my coping strategies so that I will be even better equipped in future.

CONCENTRATE ON WHAT IS HAPPENING

Having accepted what is happening and repeated the four statements above, what else can you do? If you are like I was, you will want to know what to do if you are not able to accept and relax.

Remember there are two facets to a panic attack: the physical symptoms – heart palpitations, sweaty palms, and dry mouth. These constituted 'first fear.' This is a perfectly normal response to a perceived danger and it passes with the danger.

But what usually happens next is that the phobic adds to this first fear a 'second fear' by saying things like 'I can't stand this,' 'I've got to get out of here now,' and 'God, this is terrible.' These statements serve only to increase anxiety and make you feel worse.

This second fear, as explained, is entirely groundless. You frighten yourself by saying that something terrible is going to happen. Usually you start this spiral of fear by 'what-iffing' about all sorts of potential disasters. 'What if I have a heart attack?' or 'What if I lose control?'

Once this starts to happen you get more and more tense and this makes you more sensitive to anxiety. So it's important to stop this from happening.

ESCAPE!

The first step in defusing anxiety and neutralising it is to concentrate on what is actually happening to your body. This deals with the first fear. Focus on this and forget about fuelling your anxiety by making frightening statements – none of which is true.

Allow these physical reactions to run their course. Do not resist them or try to stop them. Instead, step back and watch them as an impartial observer might. Tell yourself exactly what is happening: 'I'm panting. I can feel my heart racing. I can feel a surge of adrenaline in my stomach.' Concentrate on what is actually happening instead of filling your head with frightening statements about what might happen. Allow yourself to drift with your bodily reactions. Let them take their course.

If you allow these feeling to take their natural course without adding to them with frightening statements they will disappear in three to five minutes as your body absorbs the spurt of adrenaline that causes them. Immediately you will start to feel better. This will happen automatically provided you don't prevent it by adding second fear.

You are probably thinking, "That's fine in theory. It sounds easy but how do I stop these frightening thoughts coming into my head? It seems that they flood my mind automatically?"

The answer is to fill your head with thoughts that are helpful, leaving no room for the damaging ones. Pick one or more of the following statements and use them at the first signs of panic. Repeat your chosen statement(s) in a deliberate, confident inner voice. Do not rush it or gabble it. State it with conviction and concentrate on the words you are saying.

For the maximum effect combine your coping statement with one of the breathing exercises, such as deep abdominal breathing, outlined later in this chapter.

COPING STATEMENTS

Below are examples of helpful coping statements. The most effective statements, however, are those you write yourself or adapt to meet your specific requirements.

- This is passing.
- I am relaxing my body and floating past these sensations.
- These sensations are harmless.
- These feelings are a paper tiger.
- I can accept these feelings even though they are not pleasant.

ESCAPE!

- I am going to let this wash over me and wait for the anxiety to drain away.
- I am learning to cope with my fears.
- This is just my body reacting to adrenalin. It's harmless.
- Let go and relax.
- This cannot harm me.
- Don't resist – let it pass.
- All is well.

The benefits of positive self-talk are not confined to the phobic situation. They enrich all areas of your life. I find that having these statements on cards that I can check through gives me something to do with my hands and makes their use more effective.

The simplest way to construct cue cards is with a pack of index cards. These can be of any size. Personally I prefer the 148 mm x 105 mm (6" x 4") which are large enough to allow you to print information in bold lettering which is striking and easy to read in the phobic situation.

Self-talk is not just a matter of telling yourself pleasant things in the hope that they will somehow come true just because you repeat them to yourself. It is also about correcting the erroneous beliefs you have kept repeating to yourself and replacing them with realistic beliefs.

Take for instance your anticipatory anxiety. This is what is keeping you from entering the phobic situation. You have convinced yourself that all sorts of terrible things will happen to you even though they didn't happen the last time. Yet the fact of the matter is that all the research done with phobics and all the clinical experience of those who work with them is unanimous: the anticipation is much worse than the reality. Remember while working your way through this programme of graded exposure that you are not going to immerse yourself fully in the situations you dread – you are not plunging into it – you are gradually exposing yourself to them in a controlled way. Furthermore, you set the pace – no one is going to force you to do more than you can handle.

PHYSICAL SYMPTOMS

It is important to appreciate that there is a great deal you can do to reduce the unpleasant physical symptoms of panic.

You can eliminate the drying up of the mouth by carrying a small packet of gums or barley sugar. Sucking barley sugars is particularly useful because it releases energy, which your body can use in this situation, and creates saliva. There is also evidence that chewing diverts attention away from the other physical symptoms of panic.

ESCAPE!

If you are aware of your hands shaking simply clasp them behind your back or work through your cue cards. Some agoraphobics are very conscious of sweating during panic. Remind yourself that though you are aware of it others are not. If this is a major factor contributing to your discomfort during a panic, make a point of wearing light clothing and make sure your home is not over-heated.

The unsteady breathing, which is for many the most distressing aspect of panic, can also be brought under control. Making a conscious effort to relax your muscles will quickly restore the normal rhythm. (Several methods of doing this are detailed in Chapter 6.) Additionally you can breathe in slowly for a count of six, hold your breath for a count of six and then exhale slowly for a count of six. Continue this until your breathing steadies and the other arousal symptoms abate.

You can also practice diaphragm breathing: place your palm just below your rib cage and feel your diaphragm. Exhale slowly and notice the way the muscles move upwards. Now breathe in again and when you slowly expel the air a second time, open your mouth and make an "Ahh" sound.

Practise until you can maintain a steady, extended note by controlling the movement of the diaphragm. With a little practise you will learn to do this so quietly that no one but you can hear.

BREATHING

Controlled breathing is such a powerful method for defusing panics that it warrants a section all to itself. If you practice these procedures until you have mastered them you will have a reliable defence against panic that you can apply in any situation.

During a panic attack you 'over-breathe' and this disturbs the delicate oxygen/carbon dioxide balance in your bloodstream and it is this which gives rise to many of the distressing physical symptoms. This is called hyperventilation. There are several ways to redress this imbalance.

I'm not talking about the way you breathe during a panic attack. I mean here the way you normally breathe.

The most useful way is to redress the habit of over-breathing – which is very common among people who panic. The result of this is a semi-permanent imbalance of oxygen and carbon dioxide in the blood. This is what causes many unpleasant physical symptoms including a tingling sensation in the face, hands and limbs, muscle tremors and cramps, dizziness and blurred vision, laboured breathing, excessive feelings of tiredness and stomach and chest pains.

ESCAPE!

A further advantage of breathing exercises is that as well as addressing the physical symptoms they force you to focus your mind on something other than frightening thoughts. Soon these exercises will become associated with calmness and tranquillity and by merely starting one of them you will induce a feeling of relaxation.

DIAPHRAGM BREATHING

But to perfect this strategy you need to practice. It is also helpful to have the procedure written down on the same index cards you use for your coping statements.

When you first practise this skill you may find it easier to do lying down. Once you have mastered deep breathing in this position you can try it standing or sitting.

- ✓ Find the point just above the centre of your tummy, just above your navel. Place your open right hand there.
- ✓ Close your mouth without clamping or tensing your jaws. All breathing is through the nose. Inhale slowly and steadily, drawing the air into the bottom of your lungs. You will notice your right hand rising upwards. At the same time your chest should move very little.
- ✓ When your stomach is expanded to its full capacity pause for a moment. Then start to exhale through your nose. Breathe slowly and

steadily and at the same time imagine all the tension going out of your body leaving your muscles completely relaxed and fee of tension. Make sure you exhale fully, emptying your lungs.

✓ Each time you breathe in imagine you are drawing relaxation, peace and tranquillity into your body.

✓ Continue to breathe in and out in this manner for several minutes. Concentrate on making sure that each breath is slow and steady. Avoid snatching at the air or taking gulps.

✓ Focus your attention on maintaining a smooth and rhythmical in breathe, followed by a steady and complete out breath.

✓ Continue with this exercise for five minutes.

✓ You are aiming to take between eight and twelve breaths a minute. Breathing in and then breathing out counts as one breathe.

✓ When you have completed the exercise, notice how calm and relaxed you feel. Tell yourself that you now have a very powerful weapon for disarming panic and mastering anxiety.

✓ Remember you are working to develop a new skill, which will grow into a habit and become second nature to you. For this to happen you must practice regularly. Make use of those spare moments – when travelling, watching TV, listening to the radio – in order to totally master this form of breathing.

✓ Give yourself some prompts to remind you to practise. Putting a cross on the back of your hand is as good a means as any. Every time you notice it, it will prompt you to practise your breathing or to check that you are breathing correctly.

✓ If you practise this strategy diligently for a week or so you will be amazed at the effect it has on your sense of well being. Simply knowing you have another powerful tool for aborting anxiety before it develops into a fully blown panic attack should make you feel better.

ALTERNATE NOSTRILBREATHING

This is another powerful weapon for stalling anxiety and aborting a panic attack before it can develop. Of all the practical procedures for countering panic, this is the one I've found most effective. It is invaluable in any situation that causes you to feel acute stress or anxiety. It has an immediate calming effect. But you must practice it until you have mastered the procedure.

✓ Sit comfortably with your back straight and well supported in a chair. Make sure the chair supports the base of the back and the back of your buttocks. Release any tension from your neck and shoulders. Check that your teeth are not pressed together and your jaw is not clamped. Close your eyes.

✓ Place the tip of the index finger of your right hand between your eyebrows at the top of your nose. Let the finger rest gently along the length of your nose so that you can press your right nostril closed with your thumb. Practise doing this for a few seconds.

✓ Now release the pressure of the thumb from your right nostril and close the left nostril with either your ring finger or middle finger, whichever you find most comfortable. Practise this for a few seconds.

✓ Now try to close both nostrils at the same time. When you can move through all three positions – right nostril closed, left nostril closed, both nostrils closed – you are ready to practise alternate nostril breathing.

✓ Close your right nostril by pressing it with your thumb and exhale all the air from your lungs through your left nostril.

✓ Now inhale slowly through your left nostril. Attempt to fill your lungs during the time it takes you to count to eight. Count using 'one thousand and one, one thousand and two' etc.

✓ Now close your left nostril while keeping your right nostril closed. Retain the air in your lungs for a steady count of eight. Count the seconds silently.

✓ Open your right nostril by slowly releasing your thumb and exhale slowly and steadily to a count of eight. Aim to empty your lungs completely. You have now completed one round.

✓ Without pause, begin the next round by inhaling to a count of eight.

✓ Do at least five rounds.

ESCAPE!

✓ When you have finished, lower your hand; keep your eyes closed and notice how relaxed you are.
✓ Enjoy this feeling of relaxation you have created. Appreciate its power as a means of dispelling panic.

This technique is also beneficial if you have difficulty sleeping.

DISTRACTION

Worrying thoughts, or second fear, is a vital part of the anxiety spiral that leads to a panic attack. It increases anxiety, which seems to justify the initial worrying thoughts. This in turn gives rise to more worry, which further increases anxiety. Worry is a self-fulfilling prophecy.

One way to stop this spiral of fear is to learn to concentrate on something other than your frightening thoughts. If you do this you will not be able to fuel your anxiety at the same time.

To anyone who has ever had a panic attack, this seems a tall order. When you are in the grip of panic it seems that you lose all control over your thinking. It's as if you are trapped in a frenzy of frightening thoughts.

Nevertheless, it is possible to loosen the grip terror has on your mind and to shift your attention away from your fears. Obviously, what you focus on has to be absorbing and has to involve clear and achievable goals – anything too vague will not be sufficiently engaging.

There are three basic ways of doing this:

The first is to combine mental and physical activity. Ideally you should do some form of exercise. Vigorous physical activity is the ideal antidote to panic. Failing that tidying a room or a garage, tidy you bag or update a diary. Most absorbing of all is a crossword or other type of puzzle. Make sure that the puzzle is one you can do with a reasonable degree of effort. It should not be too easy but on the other hand do not start with The Times cryptic if you are not used to tackling it.

A second method is refocusing. This involves finding something in the immediate environment – people, the fabric of the room, the view from the window – and engaging with it. You can do this either by studying it intently and describing it to yourself in minute detail or alternatively, you can invent stories about the people or things you see. A good way to begin this is to make up the life history of whoever you focus on.

A third method is to occupy your mind with a simple yet engaging activity such as counting – count backwards from 1,000 in threes – recite poetry, prayers or lists, such as the players in your favourite team. Equally effective is imagining your special retreat. How to do this is explained in Chapter 6, Progressive Relaxation.

ESCAPE!

If you find distraction difficult or ineffective, this is probably because of one of three reasons.

Have you practised sufficiently? As with all techniques you intent to apply during panic, you need to master it under favourable circumstances before putting it to the test. Practise when you are relaxed. .

There is always the possibility that the technique is not suitable for the situation in which you tried it or not suited to your particular strengths. Try some of the others. To some extent this is a matter of trial and error.

Finally there is the possibility that when you tried the distraction technique you were already too stressed to control your anxiety. Perhaps you tried to ignore the early signs of panic or fought against them. It is important to employ distraction techniques as early as possible in the development of an attack.

When applying any of these techniques it is extremely helpful if you notice what happens to the level of fear. As you occupy your mind with distractions and turn away from fuelling your anxiety by adding second fear, the level of anxiety declines. The implications of this are significant.

What this tells you is that you can control the intensity of your panic. This is proof that you can tame it and bring it to heel. You can see that these fluctuations are affected by what is going on in your mind you are on the way to controlling your phobic reaction.

ESCAPE!

ACCEPTANCE

At this stage it is useful to look again at the importance of acceptance. The extent to which you are able to accept what is happening to you during a panic attack and allow it to wash over you will increase as you gain confidence in the phobic situation. If you are to achieve complete mastery it is important to increase the extent to which you accept the symptoms of panic.

At first acceptance may be no more than resisting the temptation to add secondary fear to the first fear. Later you will refrain from tensing up against the symptoms of panic. By taking deep breaths, relaxing and allowing the panic to wash over us, you prevent it from mounting. These are major steps and their importance should not be underestimated.

But it is possible to go further. True acceptance means welcoming those situations that provoke panic as an opportunity to practise coping with it until it no longer frightens you. Panic only disappears when you endure it in the correct way so often – by not adding secondary fear – that eventually it loses its bite.

Do not be put off by what you imagine might happen -- instead concentrate on what is actually happening. This dread melts when you confront it willingly.

Remember that you have recovered when you can cope with the symptoms. Once you have reached that stage symptoms are of no significance and will soon fade away.

EMERGENCY MEASURES

If everything else fails there are a number of guaranteed ways of eliminating the unpleasant physical symptoms that accompany a panic attack.

Take a paper or plastic bag. Cover your nose and mouth and breathe into it. Try to do this in the normal way – filling your lungs from the bottom and emptying them with slow, regular breathes.

An equally effective alternative is to take vigorous exercise. Stand upright while holding onto a table or door handle to steady yourself. Slowly lower yourself down onto your haunches and immediately return to the upright position. Repeat for as long as it takes to burn off the excess adrenaline and restore the oxygen / carbon dioxide balance.

ESCAPE!

ACTION POINTS

Reading about controlling panic is not enough. You must master these techniques by practising them before you enter the phobic situation.

Take one of the eight techniques and practise each day until you are happy that you can apply it in the phobic situation. Only then move on to learning the next one.

Make a list of each technique as you did with the coping statements so that they too are always at hand.

Having a range of techniques for defusing panic is invaluable. It means that should you panic you can abort the attack. But it is equally important to reduce your general level of anxiety so that you are less likely to panic in the first place.

How to do this is explained in the next three chapters.

Joseph O'Neill

CHAPTER 6

Meditation / Yoga / Progressive Relaxation

- ➢ Anxiety is not a permanent condition
- ➢ Meditation: the facts
- ➢ Practising meditation.
- ➢ Points to note
- ➢ Yoga
- ➢ Progressive Muscle Relaxation
- ➢ Getting the most out of PR
- ➢ Relaxation through recall
- ➢ Conditioned recall

ESCAPE!

ANXIETY IS NOT A PERMANENT CONDITION

Looking back I realise that from my early teens stress and anxiety were my constant companions. My head was full of worrying thoughts and my body was tense and knotted. I believed this was the norm and that it could not be otherwise. It never occurred to me that I had any control over my feelings or that other people were relaxed and worry-free and felt good about themselves and the world.

Meditation, yoga and progressive relaxation have shown me otherwise. They so reduced my level of everyday stress that I felt able to entering the phobic situation, knowing I could draw on the pool of tranquillity I had built up. They taught me that anxiety and apprehension are not the normal human condition. We can all attain a serenity that prevents every mishap from becoming a calamity and gives us the strength to overcome agoraphobia.

MEDITATION: THE FACTS

I know people who believe that meditation transformed their lives. Some say they only came alive when they started to meditate. Before meditation life was a trance, in which they were blind to the world.

Others make even bigger claims. Meditation revealed their place in the universe and the existence of the transcendent and gave their existence a new significance.

I am not concerned here with the spiritual benefits of meditation. If you are interested enough to explore them you will find that all the great religious traditions embrace meditation in some form or other.

In this section I deal with meditation as a means of controlling the damaging thoughts that overwhelm the agoraphobic and replacing them with a pervasive serenity.

What is the evidence that meditation can do this?

Scientists and doctors agree that meditation has a number of physical and psychological effects on those who practise it. All of these work against the symptoms of anxiety and panic.

As well as slowing down the heart rate, meditation significantly reduces the body's oxygen consumption. You remember from Chapter 5, Countering Panic, that during a panic attack the body's consumption of oxygen increases and it is this demand that triggers many of the unpleasant physical symptoms.

Meditation also suspends the activity of much of the nervous system. That part of the nervous system responsible for calming us down gains the upper hand. The result is a hypometabolic state – that is deep and prolonged relaxation. The metabolic rate slows down. This also occurs when you fall asleep but the drop in oxygen consumption that occurs during meditation is a lot greater and it occurs a lot quicker.

The number of alpha waves emitted by the brain increases. These are slow brain waves that signify relaxation and a sense of well-being. There is also a marked decrease in blood lactate, which increases with anxiety and stress. Levels fall rapidly within the first ten minutes of meditation and remain low throughout. Meditation is also effective in controlling the pulse and the respiratory rate and reducing high blood pressure and migraine.

The medical profession accepts the value of meditation in helping people to give up smoking, excessive drinking and drug use. Nor are the psychological effects of regular meditation disputed. It helps to lift depression and reduce anxiety – exactly what an agoraphobic needs. Its side effects are an improvement in concentration, memory and creativity.

On a common sense level, meditation teaches us that we can control our thoughts and shows us how to do it. It tells us that we are not helpless prey to frightening fantasies but that we can actually decide for ourselves what will occupy our minds and what we will exclude.

Perhaps most important of all meditation helps to break the stranglehold of morbid thoughts.

PRACTISING MEDITATION

There are books on every form of meditation. You will find some in virtually every bookshop. Many maintain that they offer a uniquely effective method, different from all others. In fact meditation is extremely simple and all meditation systems are essentially the same.

However, meditation is difficult. It requires patience and perseverance. During the early stages you will probably feel that you are wasting your time, that all you are achieving is a sense of annoyance and frustration. You may feel you are getting nothing out of it.

In many ways this is similar to starting a programme of exercise. At first the disadvantages seem to outweigh the benefits. In order to reap the benefits you must work through these teething problems.

The benefits of meditation are subtle. After a number of sessions you will experience little pockets of serenity. Soon these grow. Eventually you will be able to induce a state of tranquillity more profound than anything you have ever experienced. But that is not the major benefit.

That comes when the serenity you experience during meditation overflows into other areas of your life. Tranquillity, not tension, becomes your default mode. Anxiety is no longer a permanent state.

All those who have studied the medical benefits of meditation accept the following guidelines.

It is best to leave at least two hours after a meal before meditating. It seems that the working of the body's digestive system reduces the benefits.

Meditation requires focused concentration so it is better not to practise when you are tired.

To get the most from meditation you need to find a quiet place to practise, somewhere you won't be disturbed for about thirty minutes. If it is impossible to block out all external noise, mask it with soothing music. Avoid songs as the lyrics can spark off distracting trains of thought. Many people find that the sounds of nature – you can buy these on disc and tape – make a calming background.

You will need a timer or a meditation tape, made in the same way you made your deep relaxation tape, described in Chapter 6. When you have read through this section you will have no difficulty in making the tape.

First, spend some time relaxing yourself physically. You may find that immediately after deep relaxation is an ideal time to practise meditation. If not, take a few minutes to remove the tensions from your body.

Now take up your meditation position.

Ideally you should sit in one of the lotus positions. These are the classic positions used from time immemorial for the practise of meditation in the east. The position itself relaxes the entire nervous system, loosens tensions in the lower body and provides a comfortable sitting position.

Most people are insufficiently flexible to perform the full lotus position, which is an advanced yoga posture. You should, however, try the half-lotus position. If you do not succeed, persevere, as the benefits are considerable.

Remove your shoes and sit on the floor. Stretch your legs straight out. Now bend your left leg towards you so that you can take hold of the foot with both your hands. Place your left foot so the sole rests against the inside of your right thigh. Draw in the heel as close to your body as possible.

Now bend your right leg at the knee so you can take hold of your right foot with both hands. Place your right foot in the fold of your left leg, where your thigh and calf meet. Drop your right knee as near to the floor as possible. Rest you hands on your knees, with the thumb and index finger of each hand touching. Try to keep your back as straight as possible.

If this proves too difficult, simply sit cross-legged on the floor. If you find it necessary to support your buttocks with a cushion in order to keep your back straight, do so. Try to relax your body as much as possible without slumping forward. Some people find that sitting near a wall or piece of furniture, which they use as a guide to keep the back straight, is helpful. That's fine so long as you don't lean against it.

If this also proves too difficult, simply sit on the floor as comfortably as possible, remembering to keep your back as straight as possible. This position may not be immediately comfortable but it is worth persevering.

If you find sitting on the floor uncomfortable, don't worry. Sit instead in a comfortable, straight-back chair that provides good support. Uncross your legs and place the soles of your feet on the floor. Open your hands and place them, palms up, resting on your thighs.

Regardless of how you sit, always keep your back and neck straight. Imagine there is a string running upward from the centre of your head and that it is holding your head comfortably upright.

Place your tongue behind your top teeth and close your mouth comfortably without clamping your jaw. Breath through your nose.

 Now that you are comfortable you are ready to start the meditation. Eventually you will spend from twenty to thirty minutes meditating, but initially a five to ten minute is fine. Increase the length of the session by five minutes each week until you reach the desired time.

Select a focus for the session. The most popular is a word, known as a mantra, which you repeat over and over. Or the rhythm of your breathing. For the first week or so you may like to experiment with both. You will soon discover which you prefer. Once you have made your choice stick with it.

A mantra may be a word like "one", " I am at peace" or "Let go." Examples of Sanskrit mantras are "Om Shanti", "Sri Ram" and "So-Hum." Or you may prefer to choose a word or phrase that fits in with your beliefs. In the Christian tradition of meditation, phrases such as "In Him I live and breathe and have my being," and "maranatha," meaning 'Lord, come' (said as four distinct syllables – " ma – ra—na—tha") have a long tradition.

The phrase you choose is entirely up to you. You are concerned with is the sound of the word, not its meaning.

ESCAPE!

If you choose a mantra, repeat it, if possible as you exhale.

If you choose to focus on your breath, you may do this in several different ways.

The simplest is to breath in slowly and as you do so count to nine. Practice breathing in gently, without forcing or straining, until it takes you a count of nine to fill your lungs. Now exhale to the count of nine. Repeat this breathing in and out gently and rhythmically, concentrating on the count.

If you prefer not to count, you can repeat the word "one" on each exhalation, drawing the word out until you have emptied your lungs.

If you wish you can forget about the counting and instead focus your attention on the in breath and then the out breath.

POINTS TO REMEMBER

Most people find that it takes persistence and dedication over several months to succeed. It is, however, worth the time and effort. Those who seriously commit to meditation are likely to use and benefit from it throughout their lives. Of all the weapons for dispelling anxiety and controlling negative and damaging thoughts, it is the most powerful.

Remember to focus on the object of your attention, the mantra or your breathing. This is extremely simple but also extremely difficult. All you have to do is focus on the object and when you find your attention wandering, simply return to it.

When extraneous thoughts come into your mind, just let them go. You can do nothing to prevent this from happening. But you must not harbour and get caught up in them. Simply release them and gently but firmly return to the object again. No matter how many times you find yourself thinking of something else, daydreaming or becoming distracted, you simply return to the object.

It is important to adopt the correct attitude to what you are doing. Do not concern yourself with how successfully you are meditating. This is unhelpful. Do not judge yourself against any measure of success. Do not expect to suddenly feel different as a result of meditating. The changes are

ESCAPE!

imperceptible. All that matters is that each and every time you meditate you do it to the best of your ability. You will benefit from doing it, regardless of how you feel.

At all times you should adopt a relaxed and detached attitude to what you are doing. Do not try to grit your teeth and force yourself to remain focused on the object. That will only create tension and distractions. Do not become angry or disappointed when you become distracted. Accept this as an inevitable part of learning to meditate and gently but firmly return your attention to the object.

Meditation is not a competitive activity. You are not striving to reach any abstract measure of proficiency. Nor are you working to any timetable. Time is irrelevant. There is no inspector of meditation who will assess your progress and classify you as first class, average or sub-standard.

All you have to do is practise every day to the best of your ability confident that if you do you will benefit. Gradually you will find yourself becoming more 'centred.'

This term 'centred' crops up a lot when experienced meditaters discuss meditation. Like many aspects of meditation it is quite difficult to explain, though when you experience it you will certainly recognise it.

When you are centred you are living in your body. Instead of being preoccupied with worries about things outside yourself, with what might happen, you are focused on what is actually happening to you – the physical sensations you are experiencing. This sensation of being securely located in the here and now is often accompanied by a feeling that all is well with the world and that your relationship with everything is perfectly balanced and in a state of ideal equilibrium.

Sometimes during meditation you will experience this feeling. It may seem very elusive, lasting for only a few seconds before disappearing. The more you try to hang onto it, the more likely it is to disappear. It is not something you can manufacture or induce. It happens when you make yourself open to it. You do this simply by focusing on the meditation object.

It's as simple and as difficult as that.

YOGA

Like meditation, yoga has a venerable tradition. For many people it is a way of life

Here I am talking mainly about Hatha yoga, which is the yoga of the body. It lays great emphasis on developing at your own pace, taking things easy and avoiding strain and effort. It provides physical and mental relaxation, helps to keep tendons,

ESCAPE!

muscles and joints healthy and flexible and develops correct breathing.

In yoga, as in meditation, all breathing is through the nose, from the diaphragm. Push out the stomach as you inflate the lungs. This key facet of yoga is especially important for the agoraphobic.

Always breath slowly. Breathe in slowly until you have filled your lungs right down to the bottom. Hold this full breath for a few seconds and then let it out even more slowly. Wait a few seconds and then repeat slowly, without gasping.

This branch of yoga is slow and measured. It teaches you not only how to control your muscles but also helps you to develop the ability to live in your body and become centred.

I do not intend to provide you with detailed instructions on a range of yoga exercises. (The only exception to this is Alternate Nostril Breathing, which is such a powerful antidote to acute anxiety that its use is described in Chapter 5.)

As with meditation, there are numerous inexpensive books available from bookshops and libraries. (You will find a list of suitable titles in the Appendix.) Find one that deals with basic Hatha yoga – physical exercises – and work your way through it. Please read the introduction and guidance very carefully. It is very important not to strain or over-extend yourself and to progress at the pace that is right for you. Remember, you are not competing against anyone.

As with meditation, there are many classes available. There is almost certainly one in your locality. A good starting point is your local library. If they do not have details of local classes they will be able to point you in the right direction.

All varieties of yoga are helpful in that they all induce relaxation, counter stress and induce a sense of well-being. However, there are many exercises, which are especially helpful to those fighting against agoraphobia. Pay special attention to these exercises:

- ➢ Chest Expansion
- ➢ Cobra
- ➢ Neck Movements
- ➢ Complete Breath
- ➢ Shoulder Stand
- ➢ Eye Exercises
- ➢ Alternate Nostril Breathing
- ➢ Alternate Leg Pull
- ➢ Head Stand

PROGRESSIVE MUSCLE RELAXATION

As the name suggests this is a technique for achieving a state of deep physical relaxation. Of all the means of achieving relaxation this is the least known, which is surprising as it is certainly one of the most reliable and effective.

When we are anxious, our muscles tense up. This tension is the cause of headaches, backaches and many other forms of physical discomfort. It also plays a key role in producing an edgy and apprehensive state of mind, which is a fertile breeding ground for anxiety and panic.

Psychiatrists now agree that tense muscles and fearful emotions are two parts of the same walnut. If you completely relax your muscles you will experience a relaxed mental state. This type of deep muscular relaxation is also beneficial in the treatment of many conditions, including high blood pressure and insomnia. But its primary use for the agoraphobic is in the reduction of both the physical symptoms of anxiety and unpleasant, anxiety-producing thoughts.

It is an extremely effective way of inducing deep relaxation. But it has another even more valuable long-term benefit.

As you work through each set of muscles, first tensing and then relaxing, you focus your attention on how the muscles feel and the difference between how they feel when tensed and when relaxed. Once you have learned to do this you will greatly increase your sensitivity to the presence of tension in your muscles. Muscle tension is a signal that we are under stress and it makes panic more likely. Unfortunately as we usually fail to notice this we become anxious and this in turn leads to increased muscle tension. However, as you become more aware of your muscle tension you will be able to prevent this cycle of rising tension by relaxing your muscles.

The basic principle underlying progressive relaxation is simple: the best way to relax a muscle is by first tensing it and then releasing the tension.

You can get a feeling for this very easily. Place your arm on a table or worktop and clench your fist as tight as possible. Hold this for a count of five. Concentrate on the sensation of tightened muscles in your arm. Now release the tension and let your whole arm relax. Now focus your attention on the feelings of warmth and relaxation in your hand and forearm.

Notice the difference? Of course you do. But the chances are that the muscles all over your body are tense. But because you are so used to the tension you don't notice it and you allow it to contribute to your anxiety.

Like all other means of reducing stress this one requires practice. The more you practice, the more relaxed you become and the easier it is for you to spot the tension in your muscles and defuse it before it results in a distressing feeling of anxiety.

ESCAPE!

It is important to practice this skill in the right setting. For best results you need the following:

✓ a quiet room with subdued lighting, a bed, couch or reclining chair;
✓ a tape recorder. Record the instructions below onto a tape which you then play back during your relaxation session. Do this in a slow, relaxed voice pausing between each phrase at the end of each line;
✓ clothing that is warm, loose and comfortable. Remove your glasses, tie and shoes and loosen your belt.

Now follow these instructions. Do so uncritically.

Settle back as comfortably as you can.
Let yourself relax to the best of your ability.
For the present you are going to forget about anything that might be worrying you.
You are going to concentrate on my voice to the exclusion of everything else.
You will do everything I tell you to the best of your ability and you will not allow thoughts about anything else to distract you from becoming totally relaxed.
If necessary adjust your weight until you feel perfectly comfortable.
Make sure that the bed / couch / recliner is supporting all the weight of your body and that none of your muscles have to do it.
Now you are going to concentrate on one set of muscles at a time.

First you will tense them.
You will hold the tension for as long as I tell you.
Then you will suddenly release the tension, relaxing your muscles.
As you tense one set of muscles, be sure all your other muscles remain relaxed.
Now as you relax like that, extend your right arm in front of you.
Clench your right fist.
Clench your fist tighter and tighter.
Study the tension as you do so.
Keep it clenched.
Feel the tension in your right fist, hand and forearm.
And now relax.
Let the fingers of your right hand become loose and notice the contrast in your feelings.
Now let yourself go.
Try to become more relaxed all over.
Now repeat that with your left fist.
Clench your left fist while the rest of your body relaxes.
Clench your fist tighter and tighter.
Study the tension as you do so.
Keep it clenched.
Feel the tension in your left fist, hand and forearm.
And now relax.
Let the fingers of your left hand become loose and notice the contrast in your feelings.
Now let yourself go.
Try to become more relaxed all over.
Now clench both fists tighter and tighter.
Both fists are tense, forearms are tense.

ESCAPE!

Clench your fists tighter and tighter.
Study the tension as you do so.
Keep them clenched.
Feel the tension in your fists, hands and forearms.
And now relax.
Let your fingers become loose and notice the contrast in your feelings.
Now let yourself go.
Try to become more relaxed all over.
Now bend your elbows and tense the bicep muscles.
Tense them harder.
Study the tensions.
Let your arms relax, straighten them out and feel the difference once more.
Try to let the relaxation develop on its own.
Each time pay close attention to your feelings when you tense up and when you relax.
Now straighten your arms in front of you and push against the elbows so that you feel tension in your elbows, so that you feel tension in the biceps and along the back of your arms.
Stretch your arms.
Feel the tension.
And now relax. .
Get your arms back into a comfortable position.
Let the relaxation develop on its own.
Your arms should begin to feel comfortably heavy as you allow them to relax.
Now concentrate on pure relaxation throughout your arms without any tension.
Get your arms into a comfortable position.
Let them relax further and further.

Joseph O'Neill

Even when your arms feel really relaxed try to let them go just a little bit more.
Always try to achieve deeper and deeper relaxation.
Let all your muscles go loose and heavy.
Just settle back quietly and comfortably.
Now wrinkle up your forehead.
Do this by opening your eyes wide
Wrinkle the forehead, tighter.. and… tighter…
Now Stop.
Relax the forehead.
Let your entire forehead and scalp relax more and more.
Now close your eyes again and frown.
Frown and crease your brows.
Study the tension again…
Now let go.
Relax.
Smooth out the forehead once more.
Now close your eyes …
Tighter and tighter…
Feel the tension.
Now relax the eyes.
Now clench your jaws.
Clench your jaws by biting your teeth together.
Study the tension throughout the jaws..
And relax the jaws now.
Again, allow the relaxation to proceed on its own.
Now press your tongue hard against the roof of your mouth.
Look for the tension
Hold it…
And relax

186

ESCAPE!

Let your tongue return to a comfortable, relaxed position.
Now press your lips together.
Tighter and tighter…
And relax the lips.
Again, notice the contrast between tension and relaxation.
You should begin to feel the relaxation all over your face now.
All over your forehead and scalp, eyes, jaws, lips, tongue and throat.
Try to let the relaxation progress more and more.
Now concentrate on the neck muscles.
Press your neck back as far as you can until you feel the tension in the neck.
Roll your head slowly to the right.
Feel the tension moving.
Now roll it slowly to the left and again concentrate on the different feelings.
Now straighten your head and slowly bring it forward until your chin presses against your chest…
Once again look for the tension.
Now let your head return to a comfortable, relaxed position and let the relaxation develop and deepen.
Now shrug your shoulders.
Bring your shoulders right up.
Hold the tension…
Drop your shoulders and feel the relaxation.
Neck and shoulders completely relaxed.
Shrug your shoulders again.
This time move them around.

Bring them up and forwards…
And back.
Feel the tension in your shoulders and the upper part of your back.
Now drop your shoulders once more and relax.
Let the relaxation spread deep into your shoulders, right into your back muscles.
Relax your neck, throat, jaws and other facial muscles.
Just let the relaxation take over and grow deeper and deeper.
Relax your whole body as much as you can.
Feel the comfortable heaviness that comes with complete relaxation.
Breathe gently and freely… in and out…
Notice how the relaxation increases as you breathe out.
Each time you breathe out feel the relaxation.
Now breathe right in
Take a deep breath and hold it…
Study the tension in the chest…
Now breathe out.
Let the chest muscles relax and push out the air automatically.
Now continue relaxing and breathing freely and gently.
Now with the rest of your body as relaxed as possible take deeps breathe and hold it.
Now breath out slowly and notice the feelings of relief and relaxation.
Now just breathe normally again in and out, go on relaxing your chest and let the relaxation spread to your back, shoulders, neck and arms.

ESCAPE!

Just let go.
Relax more and more.
Now we'll concentrate on the stomach muscles,
the whole of the stomach area.
Tighten your stomach muscles.
Make the stomach hard.
Notice the tension...
Now relax.
Let the muscles loosen and notice the contrast.
Once more... press and tighten the stomach
muscles.
Hold the tension...
Study it...
And relax.
Notice the feeling of well being that comes when
you relax your stomach completely.
This time draw the stomach in...
pull the muscles right up feel the tension this way.
And relax again.
Continue breathing normally and easily.
Feel the gentle massaging effect all over the chest
and stomach.
Now pull the stomach in again...
Hold the tension...
Now push out and tense the opposite way...
Hold the tension again...
Once more pull in...
Hold the tension...
And now relax your stomach completely.
Let the tension dissolve away.
And let the relaxation grow deeper and deeper.
Each time you breathe out notice the rhythmic
relaxation in your chest and stomach.

Notice how your chest and stomach relax more and more.
Now try to let go of all contractions anywhere in the body.
Next concentrate on the lower part of your back.
Arch up your back...
Make the lower part of your back quite hollow and feel the tension along the spine.
Settle down again comfortably, relaxing the lower back.
Arch up your back again.
Feel the tension as you do so.
Try to keep the rest of your body as relaxed as possible.
Localise the tension in the lower part of your back...
Now relax once more.
Relax further and further.
Relax your lower back.
Relax your upper.
 Spread the relaxation to your stomach, chest, shoulders, neck, arms and facial muscles.
Try to let all of these parts relax more and more.
Try to achieve deeper and deeper relaxation.
Let go of all tension and relax.
Now flex the muscles of the thighs by pressing your heels down as hard as you can...
Tense the thigh muscles...
Now relax.
Once again flex the thigh muscles...
press the heels down...
hold the tension...
and relax your hips and thighs.

ESCAPE!

Again allow the relaxation to develop on its own...
Now press your feet and toes downwards, away from your face so the calf muscle becomes tense...
Hold the tension...
Study it...
and relax the feet and calves.
This time bend your feet towards your face so you feel tension along your shins.
Bring your toes right up ...
and relax again.
Now go on relaxing like this for a while.
Try and let yourself relax completely, all over.
Relax your feet, ankles, calves and shins.
Relax your knees, thighs and hips
Feel the heaviness of the lower part of your body as you relax more and more.
Spread the relaxation to your stomach, waist and lower part of your back.
Relax the upper part of your back, chest, shoulders and arms, right to the tips of your fingers.
Keep on relaxing more and more deeply.
Make sure no tension has crept into your throat.
Relax your neck, jaws and all your facial muscles.
Keep on relaxing your whole body like that for a while.
Now you can become even more relaxed by taking a really deep breath and slowly breathing out.
Take a deep breath... breathe in ... hold it...
now slowly breathe out.

Feel yourself becoming heavier and heavier and more and more relaxed.
Now I want you to imagine you're somewhere very relaxing.
Perhaps by a swimming pool
or on a beach in a tropical region.
The sun is warm and you feel heavy and relaxed.
You can feel the warmth of the sun on your skin.
You hear the sound of the birds.
And the rhythmical lapping of the water.
You can smell the salt air... it's the smell of the sea...you can taste it.
Put yourself in the middle of this scene and notice how deeply relaxed you feel.
Think about this scene and go on relaxing for a few minutes more by yourself, for a few minutes more thinking of this relaxed, warm place.

GETTING THE MOST OUT OF PROGRESSIVE RELAXATION

When you are deeply relaxed and picture yourself on a beach or a field, you are creating your own special haven, a sanctuary from all the stresses of the world. You will return there when you want to defuse anxiety and induce a state of calm. In order to achieve this, however, you must practice.

To get the best results from progressive relaxation you should practise it once a day for several weeks. If you do this conscientiously you will notice that you look forward to the profound sense

ESCAPE!

of relaxation you experience your sessions. More important however, is the wider effect.

At first this sense of relaxation will be confided to the actual practise sessions but gradually you will notice that you are able to extend it into more and more areas of your life. In this ways its benefits are similar to those of meditation. As you become aware of the way in which your muscles tense up when you become anxious you will find yourself automatically relaxing your muscles. Instead of getting caught up in a cycle of tense muscles and anxious thoughts, as you used to, you will respond by relaxing.

There are two shortcut methods for doing this – relaxation through recall and conditioned recall. These can be carried out virtually anywhere, under any circumstances.

First you must practice the longer form of deep relaxation for several weeks until you are happy that you can reliably produce a deep state of relaxation.

Relaxation through Recall

To benefit from this method you must have reached the stage of being able to recognise tension in your muscles and to remember the feeling of relaxation you experience when, during your deep relaxation sessions, you released those tensions.

During this exercise sit quietly and relax yourself as much as possible. Now you focus your attention on each muscle group, one at a time, just as you do when you are practising deep relaxation. As you do this, you examine it for tension. If you find any tension present, recall what it felt like when you let go of tension in that area. The muscles will then relax. Do this in exactly the same order you use when you practise deep relaxation, starting with the muscles in your right hand and forearm right through to the muscles around your shins.

Conditioned Relaxation

Conditioned relaxation depends on forming a link between your feelings of relaxation after a deep relaxation session and some cue word.

At the end of each relaxation practice, when you are fully relaxed, direct your attention to your breathing. Each time you exhale, say the word relax to yourself. Repeat this thirty times.

ESCAPE!

Practise this for at least five weeks. By doing this and saying the word relax while thinking of the deep feelings of relaxation which you are experiencing, you will find that you have given the word the power to reduce your anxiety. From then on by simply closing your eyes, taking a deep breath and saying the word relax as you exhale you will immediately release all tension in your body and feel extremely calm.

Once you have mastered this technique you will have at your disposal a powerful weapon against stress and anxiety. You can apply it anywhere, under any circumstances. It is even possible to use it when exercising. If you are jogging for instance, you can ensure that muscles not required for running are completely relaxed.

This may seem a strange thing to say as few people associate exercise with relaxation. In the next chapter I'll show you that exercise is not only a wonderful aid to relaxation but also the perfect antidote to many to many of the problems agoraphobia causes.

CHAPTER 7   THE BENEFITS OF EXERCISE

- ➤ Exercise as stress-proofing
- ➤ If in doubt consult your doctor
- ➤ Endurance Exercise
- ➤ Exercise for the housebound
- ➤ Choose an activity you enjoy.
- ➤ Start off slowly
- ➤ Excuses, excuses, excuses

Everyone knows that exercise is good for you. Every day we hear of the latest study revealing its benefits. Many of us are so sick of hearing about it that we switch off. Exercise is not for me, we say.

But the truth is that exercise is good news for you, no matter how much out of shape you are. It is one of the simplest and most effective means of reducing anxiety. This is because vigorous exercise is the most natural outlet when you are in a state of fight or flight arousal. After exercise your body chemistry returns to its natural equilibrium and you feel relaxed and refreshed.

If you are in poor physical shape you have more to gain from exercise than those who are in better condition. No matter what your age or condition there are several forms of exercise to suit you, to improve your condition, make you feel better than you could ever imagine and improve your state of mind.

In order to motivate you to take advantage of this wonderful and completely free medicine that will improve every aspect of your physical and mental health, you must first appreciate all the benefits of exercise.

Medical research proves that people who take little or no exercise – particularly if they under stress – have a far higher rate of heart disease than those who are fit. And apart from all the ways in which your physical health will benefit from regular exercise, there are many psychological benefits.

Doctors agree that exercise increases your immediate and long-term sense of exuberance, well-being, vigour and enthusiasm for living. These are precisely what an agoraphobic needs. Other benefits are that it improves your sex life, appetite, digestion and sleep. It's a tailor-made antidote to many of the ills of agoraphobia.

If you think about it, the reasons are obvious. One of the major factors keeping anxiety alive is fatigue. We are particularly prone to anxiety attacks when our energy levels are low. This is reflected in pulse rate. Pulse rate is a rough and ready guide to fitness. A nervous person in poor shape usually has a high rate – over a hundred is not uncommon. A trained athlete in prime condition may have a rate below fifty. The fitter you are the lower your resting pulse. Put it another way. The fitter you are the more stress you can stand before your heart starts to race.

Pulse rate has a further significance for the agoraphobic. The pounding of the heart that goes with increased pulse rate is for many the first sign of a panic attack. As soon as they notice it they immediately become agitated.

However, when you are fit two things happen. First, your pulse does not immediately soar as soon as you become anxious. In other words, it takes a lot more to set your heart racing as your anxiety threshold rises. The second change is even more important.

For many agoraphobics in poor physical condition increased heart rate means just one thing – a panic attack. When you take regular exercise you get used to a raised heartbeat. You come to associate it with pleasant activity, with the sense of wellbeing that exercise brings. This breaks the link between bodily changes and panic. This is a significant step to recovery.

The fit person is far less likely to react to stress in a damaging way. Exercise provides a healthy outlet for pent-up stress and prevents it from remaining bottled up and damaging.

ESCAPE!

Age or your present state of fitness are no barrier. Of course, if you are middle-aged, obese and unused to exercise, it is going to require a real commitment to get into shape. But this is not a reason for not making a concerted effort. The worse your condition, the more benefit you'll get from exercise and the less you have to do to achieve the training effect.

Regardless of your condition, provided you have no major health problems, the only thing stopping you from getting fit is your lack of resolve. Remember, even people recuperating after major heart surgery undertake a structured exercise programme as part of their recovery plan.

The body is remarkably adaptable. Called upon to perform more work it will strengthen itself to meet the demand, provided you build up gradually. Of course, this takes time. The older you are and the poorer your physical condition, the longer it takes. But it doesn't matter how long it takes. You are not competing against the clock. All that matters is that you are making a start and improving your health.

If you are prepared to invest a couple of hours each week you will reap benefits out of all proportion to the effort you invest. And many of these rewards are remedies for many of the most disturbing and intractable symptoms of agoraphobia.

Life will have more sparkle and zip. When you feel down – something that will happen less often – you will not feel as physically drained as when you were unfit. What's more, you will build up a reservoir of endurance to meet any sudden emergencies. You will feel far more mentally alert. That muggy, detached feeling that takes the edge off reality will begin to melt away.

Two reasons for this are that exercise helps you to relax and sleep better. As we saw in the section on Progressive Relaxation the best way to relax muscles is to first tense them. This is exactly what you are doing when you exercise. And this is why we experience such a profound feeling of relaxation and wellbeing after a workout.
Similarly with sleeplessness. Many insomniacs cannot sleep because their bodies are not tired, as they never exercise. Sleep induced by healthy physical tiredness is as pleasant as it is refreshing.

Consequently, you will look and feel better in an all-pervasive way. This is particularly useful in helping to boost self-esteem and nourish your eroded store of confidence.

Your weight will stabilise. If you exercise outdoors, you will acquire a glowing complexion.

Additionally, you are laying the foundations for a healthy life. You'll greatly reduce the chances of

ESCAPE!

many degenerative diseases like heart attack, stroke and emphysema.

Importantly, your self-esteem will soar. Now you are taking responsibility for your own health and becoming the sort of person you want to be. As you will be fitter, stronger, slimmer and look healthier you will inevitably feel better about yourself. You will feel empowered to overcome agoraphobia and live your life to the full.

Fifteen to twenty minutes' vigorous exercise stimulates the body's natural mood enhancers. Exercise gives you a natural high. But unlike chemically induced euphoria, this one is totally beneficial – it can do you nothing but physical and psychological good.

Regular exercise is a long-term commitment. It means a fundamental change of lifestyle. Leaving aside your determination to overcome agoraphobia, it is the best thing you can do to improve your health.

This is why it is important to get it right from the start. To ensure that you exercise regularly you must integrate your fitness programme into your daily routine. To help you do this, give some thought to the following points.

If in doubt consult your doctor.

But before you do anything, a word of caution.

If you are over forty, overweight or have been inactive for some time, or if you have any concerns about your health, consult your doctor before embarking on an exercise programme. He will almost certainly welcome your decision and offer encouragement. He will remove any concerns you might have and allow you to start exercising confident that you are taking a major step to improving your general health and redressing the harmful effects of agoraphobia.

Please, do not assume that exercise is not for you. In the very unlikely event that a structured, progressive programme of conditioning may prove harmful, your doctor will tell you. Otherwise there is no reason why you should not reap the benefits of fitness.

ESCAPE!

ENDURANCE EXERCISE

The exercise I am talking about is endurance exercise. To build up stamina you need to carry out this type of exercise several times a week. These activities are the ones that get the heart pumping and the lungs working much harder than usual. They make you to sweat.

Practical ways of doing this are:
- ✓ Walking vigorously
- ✓ Running
- ✓ Cycling
- ✓ Rowing
- ✓ Swimming
- ✓ Similar exercises, such as using an exercise bike, a step machine or a cross-trainer.

Even if your phobia keeps you housebound it is still possible to exercise

What if you're presently not able to go out?

Don't assume that you won't be able to make a start on the Initial Fitness Programme. Leaving the house to go shopping, for instance, is stressful partly because you feel that rushing home may attract attention to you. This is different. Leaving home to exercise requires you to rush home – that's the purpose of it.

Just because you find it hard to leave home at the moment do not assume you will not be able to undertake this exercise programme. Try the first stages. You now have a powerful incentive for leaving home.

You may find that it changes your attitude to leaving the house. As I explained in Chapter 1 exercise can have a profound effect on how you feel about leaving home. It removed a great deal of the fear and gave me an incentive to go out on a regular basis. Because I quickly came to associate being outside, on my own, with feelings of achievement and even euphoria, the dread quickly disappeared. From being a negative experience it becomes totally positive.

If, however, you don't feel up to that at the moment, don't worry. There are plenty of exercises you can undertake while remaining indoors.

If you are able to drive or have someone who is prepared to drive you to a nearby gym, then you should consider that option.
Most gyms now offer an assessment by a qualified instructor who will tailor a programme to your requirements. Make it clear that you are interested in improving your cardiovascular fitness and you aim to exercise for at least twenty minutes, at least four times a week.

If the gym is not a possibility or you would prefer to exercise at home, there are plenty of things you can do.

ESCAPE!

It is possible to jog in your home and – provided you do it properly – get the same benefit as you would if you did it outside. The important thing is to make sure that each foot is raised at least six inches from the ground. When jogging on the spot like this it is important that your knees are raised a lot higher than would be the case if you were jogging outside.

You can, of course, switch from indoor to outdoor jogging and back again at any time.

Use exactly the same shoes and clothing you would jogging outside, though some people believe it is good for the feet to jog barefoot indoors.

One problem with indoor jogging is that it lacks the interest of being outside where you have plenty going on around you to keep you from getting bored. One way around this is to have something – radio, television or music – to occupy you. However, if you're to get the full benefit from jogging on the spot you will have to make a conscious effort to ensure that you are raising your feet the required height off the ground. Don't become so engrossed in the music that you lapse into merely shifting your weight from one foot to the other.

If jogging is not for you – something you should decide only after giving it a try –investigate the possibility of a step machine, exercise bike or cross-trainer. Test all three at a gym. In my experience, if you explain the situation to the gym instructor he is likely to be helpful and supportive. After all, the people who work in gyms are committed to promoting an active life-style and admire those who are taking responsibility for their fitness.

If you intend to exercise indoors, you have a number of choices. You can use the jogging chart in this chapter, jogging for the time stipulated and disregarding distances. Or you can use an exercise bike, a cross-trainer or any other type of home gym. If you are using one of the latter, start off with five minutes per day adding five minutes every four days until you reach twenty minutes. In order to maintain your fitness complete four twenty-minute sessions each week.

Choose an activity you enjoy.

The choice is yours. Choose what best suits your needs as this makes it easier for you to incorporate it into your life.

There are however, certain things you should bear in mind.

It helps if you choose at least two different activities. Ideally they should be complementary. Personally I prefer jogging and swimming. Jogging works the lower body while swimming exercises the upper body. One is weight bearing, the other is not. Swimming eases the muscles tired out by jogging. Leg injuries of the type that all joggers occasionally suffer provide an opportunity to keep fit by swimming until recovery is complete. This means there is never a valid reason for not exercising.

The advantage of jogging over all forms of exercise is that you can do it at virtually any time, anywhere. It requires no specific facilities and requires only a good pair of running shoes. You don't need a partner and therefore you are not dependent on anyone's co-operation. In short, there are seldom occasions on which it is not possible to jog.

And that's an important point about any exercise programme. You must make it a routine part of your life, something you do as naturally as brushing your teeth. After a while, you will need no incentive to exercise. You will enjoy it so much that you will not only look forward to it as one of those pockets of pleasure which you have built into your day, but you will be very put out if you miss it.

But early on, before you establish a routine of exercise, you may well find it hard. At this stage you need as much help as you can to develop a routine until you become fully aware of the benefits of exercise. When that happens you'll be hooked for life.

The exercise you choose is irrelevant as long as it is vigorous enough to achieve the 'training effect' for at least twenty minutes. You'll know if you're achieving this effect because you will be slightly short of breath. By this I don't meaning gasping for breath and totally exhausted as if you've just sprinted a hundred metres. You should be slightly short of breath but able to hold a conversation. A brisk walk is quite sufficient for most people to achieve this effect.

Once you start exercising at this level you are strengthening your cardiovascular system – your heart, lungs, arteries and veins – and making it more efficient. This is the powerhouse of your body and by improving its efficiency your whole body benefits. By exercising regularly in this way you are first improving your fitness and then maintaining it.

The great advantage of jogging over other forms of exercise is that it is perhaps the most concentrated way of achieving this effect. Twenty minutes jogging four or five times a week is the quickest way to achieve and maintain a good level of fitness.

However, don't expect to go out and jog steadily for half an hour without any sort of build-up. Even if you feel you are in good shape it is wise to break into jogging gradually.

ESCAPE!

A further advantage of jogging is that you need no expensive equipment. Nor do you have to make any long-term financial commitment to get started. You need only comfortable and loose trousers or shorts, a light shirt, some type of waterproof jacket and most important of all, a pair of running shoes and thick socks.

Clothing should be loose and as comfortable and light as the weather permits. If it's cold, wrap up well – you can always take off what proves unnecessary.

The most important and expensive item is the shoes. Be sure you buy running shoes and not fashion or leisure wear. Ideally buy them from a proper sports shop that deals in sports equipment. A trained member of staff will help you choose the shoes most suitable for your purpose.

Buying running shoes represents a commitment and is an inducement to continue. They are the one piece of equipment that will reduce the possibility of injuries.

The other way to reduce aches and pains is by stretching before and after jogging. Spend about five minutes warming up before jogging and the same time warming down after.

Gentle stretching is the best way to do this. Never strain. Try touching your toes – or as far down your shins as is comfortable – without bending your knees. Place one foot on a chair, without bending your knee, and place your hands as far down your leg as possible. Repeat with the other leg.

Remember, jogging is not a competitive sport. You are not jogging against anyone. All your targets are personal ones you set for yourself in order to give you both an incentive to improve and the satisfaction of knowing that you are getting better. Everything you do is at your own pace to meet your individual needs.

START OFF SLOWLY

Exercise is a long-tern commitment. There is no rush – as long as you keep at it. Soon you will build up your stamina and improve your ability to fight off stress. But you will only slow down your progress by doing too much too soon.

Whether you are working your way through one of the fitness charts at the end of this chapter or beginning a fitness session, remember to start off slowly.

EXCUSES, EXCUSES, EXCUSES

There are a million reasons why you can't embark on a programme of exercise. Even if you overcome all these reasons and start exercising, you will then find another million reasons to stop:

you're too stiff, it's too hard, you don't have the time. The excuses are endless.

But that's all they are – excuses. They are not valid reasons. If you allow them to stop you from doing what is good for you and what will help you recover, at least admit the truth to yourself. You have decided that you are not prepared to do what is necessary to recover. You have chosen to remain as you are now.

This tendency to make excuses for doing nothing is a part of your condition. It applies to all the strategies outlined in this book. That is why I devote a large part of Chapter 10 to addressing it.

Your self-esteem has taken a battering and perhaps you feel that things will never improve. One way to convince you of this is to look at some of the common excuses we use for not exercising.

I don't have time

This is the most widely used excuse for not doing exercise and all the other things we need to do. I deal with this excuse in relation to all aspects of the programme I advocate in Chapter 10. For now, however, think about the following points.

Regular exercise requires a commitment of about four hours per week, that is four out of the 168 hours in a week. That works out at 2.38% of your week. Given all the undisputed benefits of exercise, can you honestly say that it is not worth an average of thirty-five minutes per day? That's about the length of one episode of the average soap.

By choosing the right time to exercise you can save time while increasing your chances of continuing to exercise. Exercising first thing in the morning saves time spent changing and showering. It has the further advantage that those who are new to exercise and choose to do it first thing in the morning are 75% more likely still to be exercising a year later.

By taking five minutes at the beginning of the week to plan your exercise for the next seven days you can save a lot of time. This is the great advantage of home-based exercise – including jogging – as it involves no travelling time. If you choose to use a gym or pool you can save time by going on your way to or from work.
I can't be bothered

You may feel this way because you think of exercise as a skill, needing physical co-ordination or sporting aptitude. This is not so. None of the exercises suggested – except swimming – requires any skill.

If you have no recent experience of exercise you may well have an entirely negative attitude, thinking of it as something that just gets you hot and sweaty. Once you start to exercise and experience the benefits your attitude will change.

I don't have any support

Social support, from a partner, social group or friend is very valuable. Studies with recovering heart patient show that 80% men with supportive partners, as opposed to 40% of those without, stuck to their exercise programme. If you can find an exercise buddy who will provide motivation, you have a great asset. Consider your partner and friends.

If you do not have this type of support you must work harder on all the other motivational devises.

I lack self-esteem

Self-esteem soars when you take responsibility for your health. If you wait until your self-esteem improves before starting to exercise, you will wait forever.

There are too many obstacles

Examine each of these obstacles honestly. None is insurmountable if you choose to overcome it.

I don't know how

Everything you need to know is in this chapter. If however, you feel that you need to know more, do not use this as an excuse for not exercising. Use the information in this chapter to get started and at the same time call at your local library where you will find a section devoted to heath and fitness and the various forms of exercise I discuss.

My work means I don't know when I'll have time to exercise

This means that you have to be flexible. As long as you slot in four exercise sessions, scattered though the week, you will be able to stay on track.

Use a little creativity. Is it possible to cycle to and from work? Can you exercise at lunchtime by taking a walk or jogging? Examine all the possibilities and don't be too ready to dismiss them.

ESCAPE!

Walking: Initial Fitness Programme (1)

Week	Day	Walk	Total time
1	1	Gently	20 minutes
1	2	Gently	20 minutes
1	3	Gently	20 minutes
1	4	Gently	20 minutes
2	1	Gradually increase pace each day until slightly breathless.	20 minutes
2	2	Gradually increase pace each day until slightly breathless.	20 minutes
2	3	Gradually increase pace each day until slightly breathless.	20 minutes
2	4	Gradually increase pace each day until slightly breathless.	20 minutes
3	1	Fast enough to be slightly breathless.	20 minutes
3	2	Fast enough to be slightly breathless.	20 minutes
3	3	Fast enough to be slightly breathless.	20 minutes
3	4	Fast enough to be slightly breathless.	20 minutes

To maintain this level of fitness you must continue the programme for Week 3 by walking at least four times a week for twenty minutes fast enough to make you slightly breathless.

If you wish to improve your fitness even more, you should progress to Initial Fitness Programme (2).

Jogging: Initial Fitness Programme (2)

Week	Day	Walk	Jog	Total time
1	1	1 minute – 3 times alternating with jogging	30 seconds – 3 times	4.5 minutes
1	2	1 minute – 3 times alternating with jogging	30 seconds – 3 times	4.5 minutes
1	3	1 minute – 3 times alternating with jogging	30 seconds – 3 times	4.5 minutes
1	4	1 minute – 4 times alternating with jogging	30 seconds – 4 times	6 minutes
2	1	1 minute – 4 times alternating with jogging	30 seconds – 4 times	6 minutes
2	2	1 minute – 4 times alternating with jogging	30 seconds – 4 times	6 minutes
2	3	1 minute – 6 times alternating with jogging	30 seconds – 6 times	9 minutes
2	4	1 minute – 6 times alternating with jogging	30 seconds – 6 times	9 minutes
3	1	1 minute – 6 times alternating with jogging	30 seconds – 6 times	9 minutes
3	2	1 minute – 6 times alternating with jogging	30 seconds – 6 times	9 minutes
3	3	1 minute – 6 times alternating with jogging	30 seconds – 6 times	9 minutes
3	4	1 minute – 4 times alternating with jogging	1 minute – 4 times	8 minutes
4	1	1 minute – 4 times alternating with jogging	1 minute – 4 times	8 minutes
4	2	1 minute – 4 times alternating with jogging	1 minute – 4 times	8 minutes
4	3	1 minute – 4 times alternating with jogging	1 minute – 4 times	8 minutes
4	4	1 minute – 4 times alternating with jogging	1 minute – 4 times	8 minutes
5	1	1 minute – 5 times alternating with jogging	1 minute – 5 times	10 minutes
5	2	1 minute – 5 times alternating with jogging	1 minute – 5 times	10 minutes
5	3	1 minute – 5 times alternating with jogging	1 minute – 5 times	10 minutes
5	4	1 minute – 5 times alternating with jogging	1 minute – 5 times	10 minutes

ESCAPE!

6	1	1 minute – 5 times alternating with jogging	1 minute – 5 times	10 minutes
6	2	1 minute – 6 times alternating with jogging	1 minute – 6 times	12 minutes
6	3	1 minute – 6 times alternating with jogging	1 minute – 6 times	12 minutes
6	4	1 minute – 6 times alternating with jogging	1 minute – 6 times	12 minutes
7	1	1 minute – 6 times alternating with jogging	1 minute – 6 times	12 minutes
7	2	1 minute – 6 times alternating with jogging	1 minute – 6 times	12 minutes
7	3	30 seconds – 6 times alternating with jogging	1 minute – 6 times	9 minutes
7	4	30 seconds – 6 times alternating with jogging	1 minute – 6 times	9 minutes
8	1	30 seconds – 6 times alternating with jogging	1 minute – 6 times	9 minutes
8	2	30 seconds – 6 times alternating with jogging	1 minute – 6 times	9 minutes
8	3	30 seconds – 6 times alternating with jogging	1 minute – 6 times	9 minutes
8	4	30 seconds – 7 times alternating with jogging	1 minute – 7 times	10.5 minutes
9	1	30 seconds – 7 times alternating with jogging	1 minute – 7 times	10.5 minutes
9	2	30 seconds – 7 times alternating with jogging	1 minute – 7 times	10.5 minutes
9	3	30 seconds – 7 times alternating with jogging	1 minute – 7 times	10.5 minutes
9	4	30 seconds – 7 times alternating with jogging	1 minute – 7 times	10.5 minutes
10	1	Cover 1 mile walking as little as possible	As much as possible	12 minutes
10	2	Cover 1 mile walking as little as possible	As much as possible	12 minutes
10	3	Cover 1 mile walking as little as possible	As much as possible	12 minutes
10	4	Cover 1 mile walking as little as possible	As much as possible	12 minutes
11	1		Continuous jogging for 1 mile	10 minutes
11	2		Continuous jogging for 1 mile	10 minutes
11	3		Continuous jogging for 1 mile	10 minutes

11	4		Continuous jogging for 1 mile	10 minutes
12	1	Maintenance programme	Jog 1 mile	10 minutes
12	2	Maintenance programme	Jog 2 miles	20 minutes
12	3	Maintenance programme	Jog 1 mile	10 minutes
12	4	Maintenance programme	Jog 1 mile	10 minutes

ESCAPE!

In the initial stages the distance you cover in a session does not matter. At this stage you are developing the habit of exercise and getting your body used to the stresses. All you require is a watch to keep a track of the time.

Start thinking in terms of distance when you get to Week 7. You can measure a mile route using the distance counter on a car. Even though you are not required to cover a mile within a time limit until Week 10, it helps if you train on the measured route earlier.

To maintain this level of fitness you must continue the programme for Week 12 by jogging at least four times a week. On three occasions you jog one mile in no more than ten minutes. On one occasion you jog two miles in no more than twenty minutes. This means that each week you jog a total of five miles.

Do not jog on four consecutive days and then rest for three days. It is important to spread your exercise out throughout the week.

If you wish to improve your fitness even more, you should complete the programme for Week 12 and then move on to Initial Fitness Programme (3).

This is different from the first two in that there is no walking involved – you are now jogging all the time. The only time goal you have is that you are aiming to jog each mile in no more than ten minutes.

ESCAPE!

Jogging: Sustained Fitness Programme

WEEK	DAY	MILES	TIME	WEEKLY TOTAL
1	1	3	30 minutes	
1	2	3	30 minutes	
1	3	3	30 minutes	
1	4	3	30 minutes	12 miles
2	1	2	20 minutes	
2	2	6	60 minutes	
2	3	3	30 minutes	
2	4	4	40 minutes	15 miles
3	1	3	30 minutes	
3	2	3	30 minutes	
3	3	3	30 minutes	
3	4	6	60 minutes	15 miles
4	1	3	30 minutes	
4	2	4	40 minutes	
4	3	3	30 minutes	
4	4	4	40 minutes	14 miles
5	1	3	30 minutes	
5	2	7	70 minutes	
5	3	4	40 minutes	

5	4	4	40 minutes	18 miles
6	1	4	40 minutes	
6	2	4	40 minutes	
6	3	3	30 minutes	
6	4	7	70 minutes	18 miles
7	1	4	40 minutes	
7	2	5	50 minutes	
7	3	4	40 minutes	
7	4	4	40 minutes	17 miles
8	1	3	30 minutes	
8	2	8	80 minutes	
8	3	4	40 minutes	
8	4	5	50 minutes	20 miles
9	1	4	40 minutes	
9	2	5	50 minutes	
9	3	4	40 minutes	
9	4	8	80 minutes	21 miles
10	1	4	40 minutes	
10	2	5	50 minutes	
10	3	4	40 minutes	
10	4	4	40 minutes	17 miles
11	1	3	30 minutes	
11	2	10	100 minutes	
11	3	4	40 minutes	
11	4	5	50	22 miles

ESCAPE!

			minutes	
12	1	4	40 minutes	
12	2	4	40 minutes	
12	3	3	30 minutes	
12	4	10	100 minutes	21 miles

You may well find that initially you are not able to complete three miles in thirty minutes. If that's the case, fine. This now becomes the target you are working towards. It is absolutely fine if it takes you weeks or months to achieve. You are not in competition with anyone. You are simply working to improve your fitness and while you are doing this you are not only improving your general health and wellbeing but also your capacity to defeat agoraphobia.

This programme assumes that you are jogging four days a week. You may, of course, feel that you would like to exercise more often. If so, simply move down one row on the chart each day. You should however rest at least one day every week to allow your body to recover and reduce the possibility of injuries.

Most fitness joggers believe that the optimal distance to cover each week is thirty miles. This ensures a very good level of fitness without incurring the excessive stress on the legs that leads to injuries.

In order to maintain this level of fitness, simply start at Week 8, Day 3 – 4 miles – and move down one row each day, remembering to have one day's rest each week. As you can see, each set of six consecutive steps from this point – the number you complete in a week – gives you a weekly total of thirty miles. When you have completed Week 12, Day 4, return to Week 8, Day 3 and start working your way down again.

Within a few weeks you will begin to feel the psychological benefits of exercise as you start to appreciate that your state of mind is not cast in stone but is in fact fluid.

As I show in the next chapter, exercise is just one of many simple changes which will improve your sense of well-being and reduce your general level of anxiety.

ESCAPE!

Chapter 8   Diet and Lifestyle

- ➤ Is your diet helping or hindering?
- ➤ Alcohol
- ➤ Caffeine
- ➤ A healthy diet
- ➤ Smoking
- ➤ Action Point
- ➤ Tranquillisers and Sleeping Pills
- ➤ Action Point
- ➤ Sleep
- ➤ Action Point
- ➤ Posture
- ➤ Colours
- ➤ For the Love of God
- ➤ Over-breathing
- ➤ Stress in our lives
- ➤ Action Points

IS YOUR DIET HELKPING OR HINDERING?

Not a day passes without new scientific research suggesting that this mineral or that vitamin is the answer to all our problems. Every week new diets appear each promising to transform our lives. Each new piece of research contradicts earlier research. Each new diet tells us that all the rest got it wrong.

So what do we believe?

Amid all the claims and counter-claims certain basic principles remain unchallenged. For instance, the whole scientific-medical community believes that you should keep to the ideal weight for your height because it reduces the likelihood of certain disorders related to diet – heart disease, high blood pressure, bowel cancer and late-onset diabetes.

There is also agreement that diet affects our ability to cope with stress. Fortunately for the agoraphobic, the type of diet that helps us to maintain our ideal weight and remain healthy is the same one that reduces the impact of stress.

ESCAPE!

ALCOHOL

Any long-standing stressful situation or condition carries with it the danger of heavy drinking and alcohol dependence. Many people use alcohol to bolster their confidence and agoraphobics are no exception.

The problem is that there is a strong link between over-consumption on the one hand and panic attacks and depression on the other. Alcohol is a depressant and is often the spark for the first panic attack. Many people report having attacks after heavy drinking sessions. Even where this is not the case, excessive alcohol creates many of the symptoms of anxiety – exactly the things you are trying to eliminate.

Excessive drinking also impairs your health and general well being and consequently reduces your ability to cope with stress. Total abstinence or moderate drinking is best not only for the agoraphobic but also for everybody.

Look out for the telltale signs that you are drinking too much. Developing a daily drinking pattern or a compulsion to drink every day is bad sign. When drinking takes priority over other activities, your tolerance of alcohol changes – it usually increases but then declines significantly. If you suffer symptoms of alcohol withdrawal – feeling sick, headachy, trembling, sweating, feeling tense, nervous and jittery – or find that you can only avoid these symptoms by drinking more – the 'hair of the dog' – then you should take steps to curb your drinking.

Even if none of these indicators apply, any man who regularly drinks more than eight units or woman drinking more than five units a day should take steps to reduce their consumption as they are at great risk of developing alcohol-related problems.

So what is moderate drinking? It is drinking no more than is safe.

The safe limit is twenty-one units per week for men and fourteen for women. Ideally this quantity should not be consumed in a couple of binge sessions, but spread evenly throughout the week. Doctors recommend two or three alcohol-free days each week.

One unit is a small sherry, a small glass of wine, half a pint of beer or cider; a quarter pint of strong lager; a single measure of aperitif or a spirit.

The following will help you to cut down:

- Choose one of the times when you regularly drink, such as lunchtime or early evening, and plan an alternative activity.

ESCAPE!

- Plan your day so that you are fully occupied and do not have time to think about how much you are missing your drink.
- Obviously, there are many places and situations in which you are likely to be tempted to drink. You must avoid them. It is a lot easier to do this if you make arrangements to do other things.
- When you are genuinely thirty, have long, soft drinks before you take any alcohol.
- When you are in the pub and drinking alcohol restrict yourself to no more than one drink every hour. You can make your drinks last longer by adding mixers to wines and spirits.
- Avoid drinking in rounds unless you make it clear from the outset that you are going to stick to the above rules.

CAFFEINE

Caffeine is one of the commonest stimulants found in processed food and drink. Doctors have established a very clear link between caffeine consumption and anxiety.

The main sources of caffeine are:

- ✓ Coffee
- ✓ Tea
- ✓ Cocoa

✓ Chocolate
✓ Over the counter drugs

Once you are aware of this it is not difficult to avoid these products by finding alternatives. A cup of percolated coffee has about 100 milligrams of caffeine whereas a cup of drip coffee has about 150 milligrams. A cup of tea made with a teabag that has been allowed to brew for several minutes contains about 50 milligrams.

Both decaffeinated coffee and tea are now widely available and are in many cases almost indistinguishable from the real thing. A cup of decaffeinated coffee has only about 5 milligrams of caffeine.

However, tea and coffee are not the only sources of caffeine.

- A cup of cocoa has about 13 milligrams of caffeine.
- Cola drinks are also surprisingly high in caffeine. A can of Coca-Cola, for instance, has about 65 milligrams of caffeine, as does Dr. Pepper. Use alternative drinks.
- Similarly always check the label for the caffeine content of over the counter drugs and ask the pharmacist for help in choosing caffeine-free alternatives.

ESCAPE!

A HEALTHY DIET

A well balanced diet that includes plenty of vegetables, fresh fruit, meat and fish helps both to maintain general health and build up your resistance to stress. Follow the guidelines below.

- Eating five portions of fruit and vegetables a day helps eliminate excessive salt and preservatives from your diet, which are not good for people trying to reduce stress. This is by no means as difficult as it might seem. Remember a glass of fresh fruit juice counts as one portion. This
- Liver is rich in vitamins, which combat stress.
- Avoid sweet and sugary foods, which contain refined sugar, brown sugar, honey, sucrose, dextrose and other common sweeteners such as corn syrup, corn sweeteners and high fructose. Replace the sugary desserts and snacks, which contain these things with fruit and sugar-free drinks. There is now a large range of alternatives to food containing these sweeteners. It is, for instance, quiet easy to obtain both jam and canned fruit that are sweetened with natural fruit juice as opposed to sugar.
- Make a conscious effort to replace refined and processed foods with whole and fresh foods.
- Reduce your consumption of red meat and try to replace it with free-range poultry and fish.

Eat at least three portions of oily fish – tuna, salmon, pilchards or sardines – every week.

- Drink plenty of water, either bottled or purified. Recent research suggests that we derive numerous physical and psychological benefits from drinking the optimum amount of water. You can work out how much you should be drinking by the following procedure:
- Convert your body weight into pounds
- Divide this by two
- Multiply by twenty. This gives you the amount of water in fluid ounces you should drink each day.
- Switch to whole-grain breads – most bakeries now offer a variety of these. Eat some sort of cereal every day, such as porridge or wheat or bran based breakfast cereal.
- Try to reduce your intake of foods high in animal fat and cholesterol such as red meat, gravy, cheeses, butter and eggs. Try to replace high-cholesterol oils with olive oil.
- Each day supplement your diet with a mixture of wheat germ and brewer's yeast in a glass of milk – two teaspoonfuls of the former, one of the latter in a glass of milk. They are rich in B complex vitamins, which help the body fight excess stress.
- Take a multivitamin tablet each day, a vitamin B complex supplement and a high potency dose of vitamin C every day. This will build up your body's resistance to stress and make you feel more energetic.

ESCAPE!

- Start the day with a good breakfast, which includes protein – egg, fish, meat – as well as carbohydrates – bread or cereal. This ensures that glucose is released into the system slowly over a longer period of time. Cut down the last meal of the day and build up the first.
- The aim of this is to never allow your stomach to feel empty and signal that it is hungry. This leads to the release of adrenaline – which is the cause of panic feelings. To keep the level of blood sugar steady in your circulation, avoid eating foods that are high in quickly absorbed carbohydrates such as sugar, biscuits, sweets and alcohol as they can make you feel worse. Instead try snacks such as unsalted nuts, raw vegetables, whole grains, seeds or small amounts of cheese or hard-boiled eggs.
- Do not go to bed hungry.

SMOKING

Everybody knows the health hazards of smoking. There is no need for me to repeat them here.

What you probably don't know is that smoking makes you susceptible to anxiety.

Smoking propaganda tells us that cigarettes relax you, give you confidence and help you to exude sophistication. More than anyone else Humphrey Bogart embodied the allure of smoking. He died of lung cancer.

In fact, 92% of those who die of lung cancer are smokers and half of all smokers die of a smoking-related disease.

Yet many anxious people, including agoraphobics, justify continuing to smoke by maintaining that it helps them to relax. Some even imagine that without cigarettes they will not be able to concentrate and will be too tense to sleep.

All this is complete and utter nonsense, the exact opposite of the truth. Nicotine is a powerful stimulant – it increases your heartbeat and raises your pulse, the opposite of what happens when you relax.

To make matters worse, nicotine is one of the fastest acting addictive drugs known to man. Its concentration in the blood falls by fifty per cent within half an hour of smoking and then another twenty-five per cent within the hour. The withdrawal pangs are so insidious that most smokers are hardly aware of them. They don't realise that when they reach for a cigarette it's because they need a nicotine fix.

The good news is that nicotine is fairly easy to give up. After all, millions have kicked the habit. Many complain about the pangs of withdrawal and play up the agonies they're suffering.

ESCAPE!

However, withdrawal from nicotine, unlike other addictive drugs, involves no physical pain. The worst and most challenging symptom is the feeling that something is missing. Many people complain of feeling restless but this is something you can use to help you give up.

Deciding you want to give up is the first step. Once you have made up your mind to do what is necessary to become a non-smoker you have taken the most important step.

How you decide to go about quitting is up to you. I suggest you buy one of the many available programmes and stick to it. I used the programme from Kick It!: Stop smoking in 5 Days by Judy Rosenburg and Judy Perlmutter (HP Books, ISBN: 0895864568). It covered every possible contingency and after the fifth day of the programme I knew I would never smoke again. That was in 1987 and I am still nicotine free.

Whatever approach you adopt the following should help.
- Decide that you want to give up. Decide you are going to do everything possible to succeed and that you are going to be totally honest with yourself. You will not look for excuses for smoking or try to justify smoking.
- Make clear to yourself all the positive reasons for giving up. Make a list of reasons on the form below.

Joseph O'Neill

- Look forward to the freedom of being a non-smoker. Smoking enslaves you. It deprives you of the peace and confidence you will have as a non-smoker.
- Do not start with a ready-made alibi for failure by telling yourself that you will never be able to do it. This serves only to prepare you for failure. Millions of hardened smokers have given up. My aunt who is 85 and was a forty a day smoker, who had smoked since she was sixteen, gave up smoking last year.
- Recognise that you are addicted to nicotine. Accept from the beginning that there is no such a thing as having 'just one cigarette.' No one about to shoot up heroine can claim that he is not a drug addict because he intends to have 'just one shot.' The same applies to smoking. You are either a smoker or a non-smoker – there is no middle course. And deep down, you know it.
- Yet do not exaggerate the difficulties of giving up. Most of the withdrawal can be achieved in a week and it can be complete in three weeks. Many people find that giving up smoking is extremely easy – almost painless.
- NTR (Nicotine Replacement Therapy) in either gum or patches is widely advertised and extremely popular. Before you embark on it be clear that it is only an aid. It is not a guaranteed cure for addiction and does not replace the need for willpower. There is also a great deal of evidence to suggest that this sort

ESCAPE!

of extended nicotine withdrawal serves only to prolong the discomfort.

- Avoid the company of smokers.
- Keep reminding yourself of the positive gains of not smoking.
- Remember medical advice is available at your local health practice. You need only ask to speak to someone about giving up smoking to get an appointment with a qualified health professional.
- Never give up giving up. I know a number of heavy smokers who persisted in trying to kick the habit and succeeded after several setbacks.

ACTION POINTS

Make a commitment to quit smoking.

List below five reasons (other than money) for giving up.

1. ....
2. ....
3. ....
4. ....
5. ....

Read and complete the passage below.

I realise that by giving up smoking I shall save £ per week, £   per month and £   per year. I intend to use this money to but myself .... at the end of the first week. Thereafter I intend buy a .... every week or save up and eventually buy a ....

To achieve this I will carry out the steps listed below, starting with the first within the week and thereafter the others at weekly intervals.

1. Obtain a book or programme for quitting
2. Set a date for quitting and tell everyone of my intention

ESCAPE!

3. Embark on the programme.

Signed................................   Date
....

Joseph O'Neill

TRANQUILLISERS AND SLEEPING PILLS

Many agoraphobics use tranquillisers at some time or other. They can be helpful in the short-term but they are not intended for long-term use. Despite this many people end up using them for months or even years.

The problem is that they can exacerbate the symptoms they are intended to cure. In addition, dependence on tranquillisers drains confidence because it lodges your peace of mind and security outside yourself.

If you are a long-term user, make arrangements to discuss your medication with your doctor. Explain your concerns and if you decide to discontinue your medication, agree on a programme of withdrawal.

Withdraw slowly. Do not worry if it takes months to withdraw. Giving up will improve your self-confidence.

There are a number of excellent books on this topic and a number of self-help groups, which provide mutual support. They are detailed in the Appendix.

The methods outlined in the book for helping relaxation are even more important when you are withdrawing.

ESCAPE!

ACTION POINTS

Below is a checklist of the features of a healthy diet. Number them, starting with the changes you will find easiest to make and working your way through to the more difficult ones. Each week introduce one change to your diet.

1) I do not drink (or drink decaffeinated)
    a) Coffee
    b) Tea
    c) Soft drinks
2) I eat five portions of fruit and vegetables each day
3) I eat fish at least twice a week
4) I avoid sugary foods
5) I eat whole and fresh forms of the following in place of refined forms
    a) bread
    b) rice
6) I eat a cereal every day.
7) I drink the correct amount of water every day.

SLEEP

Sleep is one of our major defences against stress. The more stress we endure, the more sleep we need. Poor sleep is a problem for many agoraphobics but it is a problem that can be rectified.

How much sleep do we need?

Most people used to think that the amount of sleep we need varies from person to person. People cite Napoleon, Churchill and Margaret Thatcher as examples of prominent people who survived with little sleep. Many people managed on four or five hours sleep a night right through the last war. It is also true that as you grow older you need less sleep.

However, recent medical research suggests that when our grandmothers said that we all need eight hours a night, they were right. We are then better able to cope with the stresses of the day, feel more relaxed and have more energy.

A few nights of poor sleep will do you no harm. Even the best of sleepers sometime go through a period of not sleeping well. You should not therefore assume that inability to sleep well every night is in any way unusual or a cause for concern.

ESCAPE!

Many things – exercise, diet, alcohol consumption and your bedroom – affect the duration and quality of sleep. Most of these can be changed to encourage better sleep.

Above all, habit plays a major part in poor sleep. A regular sleep pattern is the greatest aid to sound sleep and that's why it is so important to go to bed and get up at the same time every day. One of the major reasons why many people do not sleep well is that they are not ready for sleep having slept late that morning. Sleep, like so much in life, is largely a matter of habit and routine.

Another reason why many people find it difficult to sleep is that they do nothing to tire their bodies. Consequently they go to bed with a racing mind and a keyed-up body. The exercise programme outlined in Chapter 7 removes this problem.

We all need a period of readjustment between waking and sleeping, a period of winding down. It helps to have a fixed winding-down routine that gets you into the mood for sleep. This may consist of watching a favourite light-hearted video or playing relaxing music. Avoid serious conversations or discussing contentious issues. Dim the lights, change into slippers and put your feet up.

Avoid nicotine and alcohol in the hours before going to bed as they are stimulants and make it more difficult to sleep. Better still give up smoking.

One of the immediate advantages is that it improves the quality and duration of sleep.

Some people feel that a warm bath helps them to unwind. It is important that the water is not too hot because this stimulates the body and has the opposite to the desired effect.

Do not drink tea or coffee for three hours before going to bed. Hot milk is excellent last thing at night. Avoid cocoa.

Heavy and spicy food in the evening may stop you from sleeping. It is also best to avoid work and demanding reading last thing at night. Read something relaxing or listen to some soothing music. Do not watch disturbing television programmes or videos.

Empty your bladder before going to bed.

Before you establish a routine of sleep, it is better if you do not go to bed before you feel confident you will sleep. Go to bed only when you are tired.

Your bedroom is important. Check that the temperature is right. It is better to have the room slightly on the cool side rather than stuffy and oppressive. If you have trouble with cold feet, wear a pair of socks in bed.

ESCAPE!

Make sure the room is as quiet as possible. In the absence of double-glazing, heavy curtains may help.

Use your bed only for relaxing and sleeping. Avoid eating, drinking, reading or watching television in bed.

Lie down in bed and do your relaxation exercises or meditation. Use a tape if necessary.

Try to avoid the type of obsessive thinking and worrying about not being able to sleep that is likely to agitate you and keep you awake. Deal with the 'what if?' syndrome before it gets off the ground. 'What if I can't get to sleep at all? I won't be able to get through the day. I'll be useless at work and I'll get the sack.'

Counter that line of thinking with logic – this will not be the first time you've not had a good night's sleep and you always managed before etc. It is not true that you need a good night's sleep every night. People can go for several nights without sleep before it affects their performance. Remind yourself that lying in a relaxed state is benefiting you, resting and refreshing you.

As with other occasions when obsessive thoughts are unhelpful, it is no good trying to push them out of your head and forcing yourself to think of nothing. Anyone who has ever suffered from this type of obsessive thinking knows this. Instead have a number of relaxing things to think about. A mantra or a list of names is useful. Poetry or prayers serve equally well. Do some gentle breathing exercises – alternative nostril breathing works for me.

The only way to actively encourage your parasympathetic system to take over is to practice relaxation or meditation. Tell yourself that you are not worried about whether you sleep or not. Delight in being able to lie relaxed in your warm bed without having to get up for many hours.

It helps to pray before you go to sleep. The prayer you choose doesn't really matter so long as you place all your concerns in God's hands.

ESCAPE!

ACTION POINT

Read the following prayers. Select those that most appeal.

Into Your hands this night O Lord I commend my spirit. Into Your ears I pour out all my troubles. Into Your loving heart I humbly confide my sins and failings. Watch over me during this night, that tomorrow I may serve and praise You. Amen.

Saint Augustine left us this wonderful night prayer:

Watch O Lord with those who wake, or watch, or weep tonight, and give Your Angels and Saints charge over those who sleep. Tend Your sick ones, dear Lord, rest Your weary ones, bless Your dying ones, soothe Your suffering ones, pity Your afflicted ones, shield Your joyous ones, and all for Your Love's sake.

I most heartily thank you, O Lord, for all your mercies and blessings bestowed upon me; and particularly for those I have received from you this day, in watching over me, and preserving me from so many evils, and favouring me with so many graces and inspirations... (Spend a few minutes thinking of the good things that have happened today.) Oh, let me never more be ungrateful to you, my God, Who are so good and gracious unto me.

If after about twenty minutes you are not asleep do not toss and turn in bed. Get up and perform some undemanding task. Read a relaxing book. Then try again.

If you are still awake after twenty minutes, do the same. The point of this is to break the link between bed and sleeplessness. You may find that during the first week you have to get out of bed many times. But persist. After a week or so you will sever the link.

If you are troubled by persistent obsessive thoughts write them down during your first get up period. This externalises them and enables you to disassociate from them.

If you wake during the night make a conscious effort not to become annoyed and fretful. Everyone wakes up several times during the night. Most people, however, simply go back to sleep again and think so little of it that they often don't remember waking. The more you worry about this perfectly normal occurrence the more likely you are to have difficulty getting back to sleep.

ESCAPE!

BOREDOM

The range of entertainment available to us today is beyond the wildest dreams of even our most imaginative ancestors. We have more television and radio channels than ever before, DVDs, videos, CDs and the World Wide Web – all available without having to leave the house.

So why are so many of us bored?

Because all these entertainments are passive and they encourage us to be passive too. And passivity is fundamentally boring.

If you ever kicked a ball in the schoolyard, you will know that no televised football match can equal the enjoyment of playing. Watching the finest dramatisation of the world's greatest literature can never rival the pleasure of writing your own story or performing on stage.

Doing is always better than watching. Being a passive observer, an empty receptacle into which things are poured is no substitute for living.

Advertisers have a vested interest in encouraging passive entertainment. This is a problem for all of us but especially for the agoraphobic because the condition robs us of our confidence, inducing passivity and resulting in boredom. It is hardly surprising that life seems to lack sparkle.

To overcome boredom you must fill your time with engaging and challenging activities. This will not happen spontaneously. You have to make it happen and by doing so you are taking responsibility for your life and shaping your own destiny, a key facet of recovery.

The first step is completing the quiz below.

ESCAPE!

ACTION POINT

List five things you would like to do in your spare time.

- First list three of these that are active pursuits that require you to engage and participate rather than simply observe.

1. .... L S
2. .... L S
3. .... L S

- Now list two more. These too may be active pursuits but they do not have to be.

4. .... L S
5. .... L S

- Divide them into long-term and short-term projects, things you can do today and things that require a little planning. Circle the appropriate letter above
- Start on one of the short-term things immediately. Write down next to it what you can do today to develop your interest and do it. Next to one of the long-term interests write down something you can do in the next few days.

POSTURE

Doing things is the key to dispelling boredom and lifting our spirits. But we can also improve our state of mind when we are simply sitting or standing.

Our muscles function best when they are being used intermittently – tensed, then relaxed, tensed then relaxed. If they are in a constant state of contraction, they become tired and unproductive.

Watch a great athlete or a dancer performing, how his body is functioning to the maximum efficiency by tensing the muscles that are in use and relaxing the rest.

This is not simply a matter of conserving energy. The state of our muscles affects our state of mind. This is no startlingly original revelation – it is something enshrined in everyday speech. We talk of someone being screwed up, dragging his feet, weighed down with care, hot and bothered, up tight, or conversely, laid back, free and easy, cool and collected, walking on air, with a spring in his step. We talk about someone being a pain in the neck. These are expressions of a person's state of mind as much as their bodily tension.

As these terms suggest, there is a strong link between our bodily state and our state of mind. The two go together and cannot be separated. A tense body gives rise to a tense and anxious state of mind. We can counter this by deliberately tensing our muscles and automatically we find that we relax as soon as we release the tension. The progressive relaxation exercise discussed in Chapter 6 induces relaxation by releasing muscular tension. As you know from practising those exercises, relaxed muscles induce a relaxed state of mind. If we do not learn to release the tension in our body we will remain tense and anxious.

The same applies to the tempo of our actions. Rapid, jerky and frenetic actions sustain anxiety and tension. A simple way to let the anxiety disappear is to reduce the tempo of our actions and concentrate on what we are actually doing rather than the worrying and nervous thoughts that are preoccupying us.

Remember also that people reflect back to you the mood you project. We can help ourselves by giving out positive feelings because that is what will be bounced back at us. Try to talk in a positive upbeat way. Act the way you want to feel.

This will not happen immediately. It requires patient and constant practice.

Even when sitting or standing, the tense, nervous person's posture unconsciously screws up his muscles in a way that sustains and increases tension.

Good posture is nothing more than maintaining your position by using the fewest number of muscles.

Sitting or standing, the position of the head is vital. Check its balance: look at yourself face on in a mirror. Make sure your head is straight upright and not tilted to one side. Look at the side view of your head. Make sure it is not tilted backwards or forward. Try to find the balance and remember that the pivotal point is high up.

Use both hands to find the balance of the head. You can check that you have located the correct position by gently cupping you hand around your neck. As you move your head forward and backward you will find that the more out of balance the head becomes the more the muscles tense. Check that your head is balanced by finding the position in which the neck muscles are relaxed.

Now check your standing posture.

Without shoes, stand with feet slightly apart. Find a comfortable position with feet parallel or with toes slightly splayed. Now rock your weight backward and forward until you are conscious that it rests on the balls of your feet and your toes.

Now slowly lift yourself up on your toes and the balls of your feet and stretch your spine and neck. Hold this position for a fraction of a second and then fall back onto your heels. Repeat this several times making a conscious effort to stretch your spine and neck. Imagine that a string attached to the centre of your head is pulling you up each time.

Make a deliberate effort to relax your arms and shoulders, releasing all tension. Imagine your body stretching until it is as long and flexible as possible and all tension is gone. Think of yourself as tall. Practice this until it feels like your natural standing position.

Most of us, however, spend the majority of our time sitting at a desk. That's why adopting the correct sitting position is so important if we are to remain relaxed.

Sit well back in the seat but upright. Balance your head in the way you did when practising your standing posture. Let the rest of your muscles go slack and relaxed. Sit tall. Open your hands and lay them flat on your thighs, resting your elbows on the arms of the chair.

Obviously, when working you cannot rest your arms in this way, but you should try to maintain this position in every other respect. In particular, always sit well back in your chair with the base of the back firmly against the back of the chair. Do not slide forward in the chair.

Nor should you slump forward from the waist. Try to keep the upper back as straight as possible. Check to make sure your shoulders and jaw are not tensed up.

Finally, think about how you walk. Start with your ideal standing posture and remember to walk tall. Imagine that you are going somewhere that is extremely interesting to you and you are keen to get there without rushing. Feel a spring and lightness in your step. Try to keep your spine straight, not bent to one side.

Adopting the correct posture is one of the easiest means of reducing the tension that otherwise builds up in your body.

COLOURS

It's easy to forget how profoundly colours affect us. Imagine if everything in your home were painted black. It would not be long before you felt gloomy. To a large extent this is why so many of us in the Northern Hemisphere feel better in July and August than in January and February. The quality of daylight can lift and depress our spirits.

The same applies to the predominant colours in our homes. Cold and subdued colours have a quieting effect whereas warm, vivid and bright

ESCAPE!

colours have a stimulating and exciting influence. Certain shades of blue have a calming effect.

You can try this by getting cards of the calming colours, holding them about one foot from your eyes and while gazing at them let them blend with your thoughts. Research suggests that dark green evokes a feeling of calm, yellow joy, blue love and deep blue serenity.

Use this to your advantage. For instance, your bedroom should be full of soothing, calming colours conducive to relaxation – in other words, dark green and deep blues. You certainly do not want any bright colours.

FOR THE LOVE OF GOD

All research into the psychological effects of religion indicates that people who have faith are happier than those who do not. People of faith say this is exactly what we should expect, as faith is the result of a living, evolving relationship with God. It gives them both purpose and meaning and by acknowledging what is essentially to man's existence it makes a full and rewarding life possible.

For most, however, transcendence plays no part in their lives. This is hardly surprising as we live in an aggressively materialistic world, which is fundamentally hostile to religious values.

Despite this, many people who do not think of themselves as spiritual feel there is something missing from their lives. They are aware of a longing, which the values of modern society cannot satisfy. Some remember earlier spiritual experiences, which they have always intended to revisit. Perhaps now is the time.

Obviously, no worthwhile faith can be based solely on the desire to improve your state of mind. That's not what I'm suggesting. But if you have a latent desire to explore the spiritual dimension of your personality this may be the time to do it.

ESCAPE!

Faith, like every other aspect of our lives, needs to be nurtured. Reading is an obvious part of this. It is certainly valuable to devote fifteen to twenty minutes a day to reading uplifting spiritual material. First thing in the morning, at lunchtime or before retiring are ideal times. Check the relevant section of your local library. Most large towns and cities have one religious bookshop such as the Catholic Truth Society or the Society for the Propagation of Christian Knowledge. All large bookshops have a religion section. Some relevant books are listed in the appendix.

But as with so many other things, faith is best developed by interaction with others. By regular participation in a church or other spiritual organisation you will deepen your commitment. Regular practice of meditation and prayer are both ideal ways to develop your spiritual life.

This is not a substitute for the practical strategies outlined in this book. But you may find that it helps to put your life in context and gives you a fresh outlook.

OVER BREATHING

The importance of correct breathing has cropped up repeatedly throughout this book. It is a key element in Chapter 9, the most important part of the book

Though over-breathing can produce all the symptoms of anxiety, the problem is not necessarily obvious. Over-breathing does not usually involve gasping or panting. Yet it is still possible that you are taking too much oxygen into your system and by upsetting the balance of oxygen in your blood producing the symptoms of anxiety. The commonest telltale signs that this is so are tightness in the muscles and feeling dizzy and unwell.

Ideally you should breath from your diaphragm and not the top of the lungs.

Check your breathing periodically throughout the day and remind yourself how you should be breathing. Whenever you get a minute, place your right hand on your abdomen and practise a few deep breathes. As you breathe in, your hand should rise up. As you exhale it falls.

Checking acts as a corrective.

ESCAPE!

STRESS IN OUR LIVES

Stress is an unavoidable part of life. You are not the only person who has a stressful life and you have no right to expect a stress free life. In fact such a life would be extremely boring and although it might seem very appealing to a person whose life seems to be a torment of anxiety such a flat existence would be depressing.

Unnecessary stress, the type that wears you down and leaves you feeling drained without any compensating reward is a different matter. That stress is entirely negative and we should eliminate it from our lives.

The most dangerous form of arousal is when it is combined with emotions of hostility, aggression or the threat of defeat. These feelings cause an excessive release of the hormone noradrenaline, which raises the blood pressure and results in cholesterol being laid down in the blood vessels. This leads to thickening and damage to the walls of the arteries.

The ancient teachers who advocated the virtues of acceptance, compassion and turning the other cheek were indeed wise, as these sentiments are the ones that take the least toll on our nerves and body.

Fostering physical and mental relaxation in the ways explained is the most effective way of stimulating the parasympathetic nervous system which is key to reducing arousal, lowering blood pressure and slowing the heart rate as well as helping to heal any damage already suffered.

By being more relaxed in day-to-day living we save energy, increase our well-being and reduce sleeping problems. It also helps to lessen the ill effects of worry by blunting our sensitivity to troubling thoughts.

ESCAPE!

ACTION POINTS

Run through the following anti-tensions drill at least five times a day. It will make you aware of the ways in which you are creating avoidable stress and tension.

- Check that your jaw is not clenched
- Check that your fist is not clenched – fingers should be uncurled
- Sit not on the edge of the chair but well back with your back supported against the back of the chair
- Let your shoulders drop – feel how this removes tension
- Make a conscious effort to breathe from the bottom of your lungs – not from the top. Put your hand on your stomach and feel the stomach swell as you breathe in and shrink as you breathe out
- Move your head around to make sure that it is properly balanced – check this by putting your hand on the back of your neck and feel the muscles relax
- Let your knees roll outwards and stretch yours toes making sure they are not curled up in your shoes
- Replace any negative thoughts you have with positive one. Concentrate on how relaxed you feel – immerse yourself in this feeling. Congratulate yourself on having achieved this feeling and make yourself fully aware of how it

feels. It is extremely enjoyable and certainly worth the few minutes it has taken you to achieve.

- Make a conscious effort to check yourself for tension in an hour's time. When you feel yourself becoming tense or become aware of negative thoughts your automatic response should be relaxation. Do not start telling yourself you feel tense – tell yourself this is a signal for you to relax.
- Remember you are learning to relax – tension is not something over which you have no control. How you respond to it is entirely a matter of choice. It requires patience, perseverance and determination to make relaxation and not tension your default mode.

Now that you have at your disposal a range of techniques for reducing everyday stress you are prepared to get to grips with the heart of agoraphobia. Everything so far has been a preamble to entering the phobic situation, described in the next chapter.

CHAPTER 9   Progressive Desensitisation

- ➢ The heart of the matter
- ➢ Avoidance and reinforcement: breaking the cycle of fear
- ➢ Can I do this?
- ➢ Drawing up a list
- ➢ Organising a hierarchy
- ➢ Action point
- ➢ Using your hierarchies
- ➢ Desensitisation in imagination
- ➢ Entering and staying the phobic situation

THE HEART OF THE MATTER

This and the next chapter are the most important in the book. They describe what all those who work with agoraphobics agree is the only way to overcome your fears.

Read these chapters carefully. Then read them again. Before you begin to practise progressive desensitisation it is vital that you have a clear understanding of the procedure and know exactly what you must do at each stage.

AVOIDANCE AND REINFORCEMENT: BREAKING THE CYCLEOF FEAR

As I explained earlier, the avoidance that resulted from your first panic attacks started the vicious cycle of fear that led to your agoraphobia. Because you associated certain situations – lifts, shops, public transport – with panic attacks, you started to avoid them. Every time you did that you unwittingly increased your dread of those situations and made them even more frightening

Even worse, you started to develop fears that had nothing to do with where you suffered your original panic attack. So if your first attack was in a lift, for instance, you began by avoiding lifts but soon

ESCAPE!

discovered that other confined spaces also caused you problems. Once you added these to the places you avoided, you invested them with the power to trigger the fear response, so that the scope of your fears grew and grew.

Progressive desensitisation reverses this process. Instead of avoiding fearful situations, you learn how to expose yourself to them gradually, in a controlled and structured way. As you do this you learn that you are capable of staying in the phobic situation without fear overwhelming you.

Each time you do this you are learning that fear is not the inevitable response to the phobic situation. The more often you enter the phobic situation, the less fear you experience, your confidence grows until eventually your anxiety disappears.

At this stage of recovery you will find that the generalising effect that caused your fears to grow as your agoraphobia developed, is now working to your benefit. Now you experience a benevolent generalising, a halo effect: as the particular phobia you are working on begins to improve, other fears start to diminish too.

CAN I DO THIS?

Many of you hearing of this method for the first time are already feeling anxious at the thought of entering the phobic situation. Some of you are probably even thinking of rejecting the whole idea out of hand.

'If it were possible for me to enter the phobic situation without panicking,' you're saying to yourself, 'I wouldn't have a problem and I wouldn't be reading this book in the first place!'

Let me make a few things clear.

This strategy does not involve you plunging headlong into all the situations you dread. There is such an approach to tackling phobias. It is known as 'flooding'. But that's not what I'm advocating.

What I'm talking about is gradual exposure. This means that you start off with those situations that you find only mildly uncomfortable. When you have learnt to tolerate these situations without anxiety, then – and only then – do you progress to a more difficult situation.

This strategy is structured. You progress from the situation you have mastered to one that is only slightly more difficult. You are not required to make massive leaps from 'easy' to 'extremely difficult' challenges.

ESCAPE!

This is why compiling your hierarchy of phobic situations, which we will tackle shortly, is so important. It is central to the whole programme of recovery.

And remember you are not going into these situations unarmed. You are no longer a passive victim, waiting for panic to strike. Should you require them, you have at your disposal a number of techniques for defusing and controlling anxiety. Now you know what to expect and how to deal with it.

Moreover, you also have a range of strategies to ensure that you tackle these challenges in the right frame of mind. Even before you enter these situations you will have used your progressive relaxation sessions (described in Chapter 6) to visualise a successful outcome. Finally, you have enlisted a helper to support you when you feel it necessary.

This is not to say you won't encounter difficulties. But none of them is insurmountable.

The first step is to draw up a complete list of all the situations you dread.

DRAWING UP A LIST

Take a large sheet of paper and write down every situation you avoid or find difficult. It is important that your list is as complete as possible. Do not omit things because you find them only slightly difficult. Be sure to include things you don't do any more and perhaps haven't done for many years because you fear they will cause you to panic.

Put them down in any order, just as they come into your head. Use the following prompts to help you write a complete list.

Situations you avoid: checklist

- ✓ Confined spaces: lifts, small rooms, crowded rooms, shops, cinemas / concert halls, sports arenas.
- ✓ Transport: buses, trains, ferries, aeroplanes.
- ✓ Being away from home: in the street, in the home of member of the family, in a friend's home, in a hotel with family, alone in a hotel, in this country, abroad.
- ✓ Social situations: in a restaurant, at a party, at the home of friends, giving a talk to a group of people.
- ✓ Isolation: alone in the house, alone in someone else's house, alone in a public

ESCAPE!

place, alone during the day, alone overnight, alone for a week end.

These prompts are not applicable to everyone. Nor are they exhaustive. There may be whole areas of your life that you find difficult, which are not mentioned. List these too.

Take as much time as you need to complete this task. Try to be as specific as possible. So, if you find going to the cinema a problem, especially if you have to sit in the middle of a row, put this in your list. But also add similar situations that you find slightly easier, such as "Going to the cinema and sitting at the end of the row near the exit," or "Going to the cinema when the auditorium is fairly empty and I feel I can get out quickly." The more detail you include, the more specific you are about each situation, the better.

You may find the Definition, Symptoms and Checklist of Symptoms sections of Chapter 1 also provide useful prompts.

Return to your list repeatedly over the next few days as more things occur to you. If you have been agoraphobic for some time there will be situations you have avoided for so long that you may not be immediately aware that you avoid them.

This list is the foundation stone on which the recovery programme is built. It is therefore essential that it include every problem area.

ESCAPE!

ORGANISING A HIERARCHY

Now that you've completed your list, look over it with a view to organising your points under a number of headings, so that each phobic situation is grouped with similar ones.

You may find the prompts above useful. Many agoraphobics have one cluster of fears relating to travel another relating to being alone and yet another to being away from home. If so, use these headings together with any others that occur to you. If not, work out your own headings and organise all your points under them.

Now look at each grouping one at a time. Try to organise the points in order of difficulty, starting with the situation you would find easiest to tackle and working your way through until you come to the most difficult situation.

Ideally, you should have about ten points in each list. More is fine, but fewer may be a problem. If you find that you have less than ten, look at your list again. Make sure you have missed nothing out.

If you still can't think of anything to add, try refining your list. For instance, if you have 'Going in a lift' as one of your points, try to break it down into more specific situations such as 'travelling in a lift for one floor on my own', 'travelling several floors in a crowded lift,' 'travelling in a lift I know' or 'travelling in a lift I don't know.'

Remember, your hierarchies should:

✓ include all the phobic situations that cause you a problem of any sort, no matter how minor;
✓ each contain similar problems;
✓ each include at least ten situations, each described in as much detail as possible;
✓ start with the one that is least difficult for you to tackle and work up to the one that is most difficult;
✓ be arranged so that the increase in difficulty between each step and the next is equal or as near equal as possible. For instance, assume you have a problem with public transport and have avoided buses for some time. You may decide to have a hierarchy dealing entirely with buses. Your first step might be something like 'Getting on a bus with a helper and travelling downstairs for one stop.' Perhaps your second step might be 'Getting on a bus with my helper waiting at the bus stop while I travel alone downstairs for one stop.' If your third step is 'Travel alone on a bus from London to Glasgow,' then this is clearly a far bigger step up than that between your first and second steps. In this case you need to put a number of steps in between the second and third steps.

When you are confident your hierarchies meet all these criteria turn to the Appendix and find the sheet Hierarchies. There are several of these but if you need more simply photocopy them.

ACTION POINT

Now fill in each sheet. (See Appendix) It is better if you do this in pencil. No matter how good they are you may have to alter them at some stage in the future.

USING YOUR HIERACHIES

The hierarchies you have drawn up are your master plan. You are now ready to begin working your way through each of these situations.

Which hierarchy you begin with is entirely up to you, though it is advisable to start with the one you find easiest. When you have decided on which situation you intend to tackle first, you should begin to prepare yourself.

The first step is to define exactly what it is you are going to do. You must be very precise, deciding what you are going to do, where, when, for how long and under what circumstances.

For instance, if you begin by tackling your phobia of buses, you could define your task as 'I am going to travel with my helper for one stop on the bus from the end of my street to High Street. I will do this on Sunday morning when the bus will not be crowded.'

DESENSITISATION IN IMAGINATION

The second and most important aspect of your preparation is visualisation. This is known as desensitisation in imagination. Though very simple this is a technique that will make it easier for you to cope with the phobic situation.

Use the progressive relaxation technique (described above in Chapter 6) to reach an extremely calm and untroubled frame of mind.

When you are completely relaxed, visualise your peaceful sanctuary with which you conclude your progressive relaxation exercise. Don't just think about it: spend some time getting yourself inside the situation. Use all your senses to create a powerful feeling of being in this secure and comfortable place where you feel content and relaxed.

It's very important that before you start visualising the phobic situation you are completely relaxed. Otherwise you will not get maximum benefit.

Once you have achieved this and you feel comfortable and tranquil, imagine yourself in the

ESCAPE!

phobic situation, starting with the first rung on the hierarchy. Take it one stage at a time, as in the example below.

Try to imagine yourself within this situation. Experience it as vividly as possible making yourself aware of every detail.

See yourself in the scene. You are calm and composed, handling the situation with confidence. It is essential that you imagine the scene as vividly as possible, in the same detail as you imagined your place of sanctuary. It is important to impress the scene on your senses. The following help:

- ◆ Focus on the people in the scene. Notice what they look like.
- ◆ Visualise all the objects in the scene. Notice what they are made of and their colour, size and shape.
- ◆ See yourself clearly. What clothes are you wearing?
- ◆ Examine the sensations you feel in the different parts of your body. Feel your clothes against your skin.
- ◆ Describe the quality of the light. Is it dull, bright, gentle or harsh? Is it natural or artificial light?
- ◆ What sounds do you hear? If there is music listen to it.
- ◆ What is the temperature?
- ◆ What can you smell?
- ◆ Is there a taste in your mouth?

Now go through the scene frame by frame

❖ First you see yourself approaching the bus stop. You are calm, relaxed and perfectly confident.

❖ The bus pulls up and you remain tranquil. It stops and you get on and take your seat. You are completely unruffled. In fact, you feel elated, proud of what you have already achieved.

❖ You see yourself remaining perfectly serene as the journey progresses. Think of all the positive thoughts that fill your head as you sit on the bus. You see yourself looking out the large windows, watching pedestrians, seeing the houses as you pass by. Everything you see is fascinating, occupying your mind with pleasant thoughts.

❖ You see yourself becoming more and more relaxed as the journey progresses.

❖ Finally, you approach your stop. You are disappointed because you are enjoying the experience. The bus comes to a stop and you get off.

❖ You are elated, proud of what you have achieved. What's more, you are looking forward to your next bus journey so you can build on this triumph.

When you can visualise one stage while remaining perfectly calm, you are ready to progress to the next one. Proceed in this way until have visualised

ESCAPE!

the whole journey while remaining calm and relaxed.

If at any stage during the visualisation you start to feel anxious, employ the coping strategies you have learnt to reduce your anxiety. Use your abdominal breathing and your coping statements. Keep on doing this until your anxiety starts to decline. See yourself coping quite competently with your fears, bringing them under control and remaining happily in the phobic situation.

After you have spent a minute visualising yourself in the phobic situation, return to your warm, secure scene in which you are fully relaxed. Get yourself back into a state of total relaxation again. Take as long as necessary to become fully relaxed once more.

Now once more, visualise yourself in the phobic situation. Place yourself right in the centre of the situation and really experience it again. Remain there for one minute. Then return to your place of sanctuary.

Keep alternating between the two scenes until you are able to see yourself in the phobic situation without experiencing more than a mild twinge of anxiety.

The more often you go through this exercise and the more intensely you see yourself in the phobic situation while remaining relaxed and calm, the better. Each time you visualise the phobic situation its capacity to elicit anxiety is less than on the previous occasion. Remember, do not return to the phobic situation until you have become completely relaxed. It is important that you do not enter the imagined situation in an anxious state. The calmer you are in your visualisation, the easier it will be for you to project that sense of composure into the real situation.

It may happen that visualising the phobic situation causes you to suffer very strong anxiety. If this is so, withdraw from the situation. Do not allow your stress to spiral. Return immediately to your sanctuary and allow yourself to become relaxed.

Now return to the phobic situation and remain there for only a short time before returning to your sanctuary. Keep on alternating, staying in the phobic situation for only a short time, until you find that you are able to visualise a confident and calm you coping with the situation. If, before you get to that stage, you feel only manageable anxiety, then practise your coping strategies to bring your stress down to a low level.

A session such as this should last for about twenty to thirty minutes. If you practice visualisation every day, you will get the maximum benefits. A regular pattern of practice is important.

This preparation is extremely valuable. While it is not intended to be a substitute for actually experiencing the phobic situation it is the next best thing. In a sense, it is half way between planning to tackle the situation and actually doing it. It is a gradual step towards the situation you are about to confront and consequently it makes it easier to confront it.

But it does far more than that. It is the first step to desensitising you to the phobic situation – enabling you to confront it without being overwhelmed by panic. Already you have seen yourself in that situation while remaining perfectly calm and composed. You have proved to yourself that you can change the way you think about the situation and by doing that you are altering the way you react to it.

There is another piece of good news. In my experience the reality of a phobic situation is always less stressful than my visualisation of it. Whether this is because the visualisation works very well in reducing the impact of the real situation or because agoraphobics are pessimistic about most things, including the outcome of their plans for tackling phobic situations, I don't know. But from my experience, the reality is always easier than I anticipated.

In order to allow you to concentrate fully on visualisation, it helps if you put the instructions on a tape, just as you did for progressive relaxation (Chapter 6). You will find the following outline helpful.

- Copy the instructions for deep relaxation. Many people find that it is most effective and time-efficient to practice visualisation immediately after deep relaxation.
- Imagine yourself in your sanctuary. Develop a powerful feeling of security and tranquillity. Describe the scene, pausing frequently.
- Describe yourself, in vivid detail, entering the first phobic situation. Visualise yourself there.
- Allow 25-30 seconds of silence.
- Now prompt yourself to relax further in this situation.
- Allow 30 seconds of silence to pass.
- Visualise yourself as calm, relaxed and confident in the situation. If you think some abdominal breathing would help at this stage, inhale a slow, measured breath. As you exhale, feel all the tension leaving your body, leaving you feeling totally composed.
- Allow 25 to 30 seconds of silence to pass.
- Now instruct yourself to return to your sanctuary. Describe it and the feelings you associate with it.
- Allow a minute of silence to pass.
- Now visualise yourself returning to the phobic situation.

Continue alternating until the tape has run for about thirty minutes.

ESCAPE!

If at any time you find that you need more time that the tape allows to return to a fully relaxed state, simply stop the tape and take as much time as you need.

An important part of preparation is deciding if you are going to enlist the support of your helper in tackling this particular task. In making this decision, you should bear in mind the following points.

It is better not to use a helper if you feel it is possible to tackle the situation alone. Remember, if you do enlist the support of a helper, you must include this in the description of your task, which you enter in your log (attached in appendix). The task now becomes 'I travel for one stop on the bus from the end of my street to High Street. I do this with my helper on Sunday morning when the bus is not crowded.' The original task, to make the journey without a helper, now becomes a separate task, which you will tackle at a later date.

However, if you feel the need to enlist your helper, you should certainly do so.

Finally, set yourself a specific date and time for your first practice. And make sure you stick to it.

Now you are ready to begin practising each of the situations in your hierarchy. As you do so, remember the following points.

On each occasion you work on your hierarchy, try to achieve exactly what you set out to do. Do not attempt something more difficult and do not change your mind at the last moment and do something else.

Remember that the longer you remain in the phobic situation, the more your fears subside. This will happen quite naturally, without you having to do anything. This is why it is so important that you remain in the phobic situation for as long as planned. By doing this you are learning how to control your fear.

The more often you repeat the task you have set yourself, the easier you will find it and the more you will conquer your fears. If you have sufficient time, after you have completed your bus journey, you should walk back to where you boarded the bus and repeat the exercise. The more often you do this within a single practice session, the more benefit you get.

ESCAPE!

ENTERING AND STAYING IN THE PHOBIC SITUATION

When you get on the bus give yourself time to adjust to the situation. Have confidence in your ability to cope with small surges of anxiety by using relaxation. Now take in your surroundings. Look all around you. Notice things in as much detail as possible. Observe what is going on. What the weather is like, who is present. Listen to the sounds. Smell and touch your surroundings. Take it everything.

There are many ways in which you can do this by involving yourself in reassuring activities. Some of these are:

- ✓ reading signs to yourself
- ✓ counting cars or people
- ✓ reciting
- ✓ talking with your helper
- ✓ reading the addresses and telephone numbers in your memo book
- ✓ working on a crossword puzzle
- ✓ chewing
- ✓ reading
- ✓ observing the colours and textures of people's clothes
- ✓ counting forwards and backwards
- ✓ listening to music
- ✓ doing relaxation drills.

Absorb everything. As you slowly proceed continue to notice details of your environment in a very deliberate way. You will find that this is an especially effective procedure for dealing with anxiety situations from which escape is impossible.

Study your cue cards and silently repeat the positive self-talk statements.

If your helper is with you make sure that you use him only in ways that will help your recovery. His role is to support and encourage. But he must not help you to carry out escape or avoidance behaviours. If you suggest leaving the situation he should say, 'Wait a few moments. Use your relaxation drills. You will start to feel better soon. Anxiety subsides on its own. Breathe your anxiety away.'

Of course, it is important that you have previously explained to the helper exactly what his role involves and what is not helpful.

I think it is best to have a complete timetable of things to do. You can have them written down in a book and go through them systematically. Your list could be something like this:
1. Absorb the surroundings.
2. Do abdominal breathing exercises.
3. Distract myself by talking.
4. If necessary work on a crossword puzzle.

ESCAPE!

By using these techniques you are able to remain in the phobic situation while you gain control of your fears. Your feeling of helplessness is changing as your confidence develops. This will reduce your fear and make the next step easier.

You should not expect your fear to disappear immediately. Do not be disappointed when you find that anxiety is still present. Your goal in the early stages is to function with a degree of anxiety. Later this will diminish and eventually you will be able to enter the phobic situation with little or no fear.
You should also expect that when everything seems to be going very well and the fear is steadily reducing, suddenly you will experience a spurt of fear. This can be demoralising and may give you the impression that all your progress has disappeared and you are back to square one. Not so.

Your progress will become evident as you repeat each step in the hierarchy.
Repetition is needed to firmly establish your ability to function in the phobic situation. Practise every situation several times, until you are perfectly happy with it.

By confronting the phobic situation you have placed your foot on the first rung of the ladder of complete recovery. In the next chapter I'll discuss some of the ways in which you can keep your eyes focused on the pinnacle and avoid being diverted from your goal.

CHAPTER 10   Making & Maintaining Progress

➤ Making a start
➤ Keeping On
➤ Overcoming Obstacles

MAKING A START

You developed agoraphobia by escaping from unpleasant situations and then avoiding them. Each time you did this you rewarded yourself for flight and avoidance. Now you can use the same principle of reward that led to your phobia to eradicate it.

You may understand this perfectly well yet feel so bad that you think you are incapable of making a start. The lower you are, the more isolated you are, the more difficult it is to motivate yourself. If you're very low it's easy to think the best you can do is get through the day without a panic attack. Anything else, you tell yourself, is beyond you.

This is a major problem when you're down – it's as if your willpower is paralysed. This too forms one of these vicious circles we keep encountering. Because you feel down, you don't feel like doing much so you restrict your activities more and more. This reduces the amount of stimulation and interest in your life, which consequently makes you feel worse. Because you are doing so little you feel bad about yourself.

Doing anything positive to improve your condition will make you feel better. And the more you do, the better you will feel.

At the moment you are caught in a cycle of despair and stress. As long as you stay on that treadmill nothing will change. You may think that you are never going to feel any better.

But these feelings, no matter how convincing they might seem, are to a large extent the result of what you are thinking and what you have been saying to yourself. You've probably been saying these things for so long that you are totally unaware of the message you are constantly reinforcing. As you've seen, once you change what you say to yourself, the way you feel will start to change.

But what will change your feelings profoundly and rapidly is a change of behaviour. Once you start to confront your fears your attitude to them will begin to change. You have to challenge your acceptance of your condition. You do that by embarking on a programme of recovery.

So how do you make a start?

ESCAPE!

Think about what you have to do to start tackling your agoraphobia. Ask yourself how you feel about the prospect of tackling these things and what obstacles you see. Be totally honest. Is laziness or fear of changing the pleasant parts of your lifestyle an obstacle?

ACTION POINT

Write down each of the genuine obstacles in as much detail as possible.

Now check your list against the following points below.

i.   When you are down you are so frozen in the present moment that you forget that you ever felt better and can't believe that you will feel better in the future.   Part of the problem is that you cannot believe that things can be better in the future. Let me tell you something that happened to me recently that made me realise that it is possible to feel better than you have at any time in your life.

Believe it or not, I do practise what I preach. Several weeks ago as I lay in bed, about to fall asleep, I was reminding myself of all the good things that had happened to me that day. I was in Italy at the time, enjoying an idyllic holiday. The intensity of my pleasure was due to the twenty-five years during which I had avoided boats and trains and consequently not taken holidays.

That day I had enjoyed a wonderful run along the shore of Lake Garda, something I was able to do only because I had taken up exercise and given up smoking to help control my panics.

Suddenly it occurred to me that so many good things in my life were the result of deciding to overcome agoraphobia. If I hadn't tackled my fears I would have none of those things that are today such a joy.

Take the first step – the first in vivo situations. But take it slowly.

ii. Rushing will only increase your tension. Remember it is important to act as if you feel calm and relaxed. Walk in a leisurely fashion, taking in your surroundings, talk in a calm, measured way without whispering or raising your voice and behave at all times like someone who is self-possessed. You may feel anything but relaxed but acting as if you are will help you to get into that frame of mind.

iii. Do not fool yourself by saying that you do not feel like starting now and that you will wait until you do feel like starting. You know perfectly well that this is just an excuse and that you will never feel like it if you simply

ESCAPE!

sit around waiting for things to change on their own.

Your fears will only disappear when you desensitise yourself to the phobic situation. By constantly exposing yourself to situations that provoke anxiety and by managing that anxiety, you will reduce the severity of the phobic reaction until you are able to control it totally.

Only you can cure your agoraphobia. No matter what help and support you have, ultimately it depends on you. It is not easy. It requires determination, commitment and persistence.

The secret is to break the problem down into small, manageable parts, which you deal with one at a time. This is what this book does.

As the Chinese say, 'A journey of a thousand miles begins with a single step.'

KEEPING ON

Do not put additional pressure on yourself by working to an unrealistic timetable. As long as you are devoting at least two sessions every week to practising in vivo desensitisation you are making progress. For so long as you are putting yourself into the phobic situation and learning to control the resulting anxiety, you are moving along the path to total recovery. Repeated exposure to a situation you find threatening reduces the severity of the symptoms you experience in that situation. It happens automatically. Your aim is to help it along.

Remember that it is perfectly normal to experience an increase in anxiety during the initial stages of recovery. This is because you are abandoning the safety of a cosseted lifestyle and starting to confront and overcome your fears. The important difference is that this time you have at your disposal an array of strategies for disarming and conquering fear.

At this stage of recovery it is tempting to believe that it is better to accept your illness and put up with it. Doing nothing is always the easiest course of action. The world is full of long-term agoraphobics who have decided to do nothing. Many of them are confined to their homes. This is why you have to make a commitment to recover and why you have to constantly reaffirm it. You reaffirm it by following the programme of recovery – by not deceiving yourself, by not pretending you are confronting your difficulties if you are not repeatedly entering into phobic situations. Be honest with yourself.

If you do nothing or make a half-hearted effort, that is your choice. Like all choices it entails certain consequences.

ESCAPE!

Be tenacious – like the little dog that has hold of the burglar's trouser leg. Be systematic. Don't try to take short cuts – there are no short cuts.

Be aware of the problems memory may cause. To a large extent the tense and vulnerable attitude of the agoraphobic is the result of memory and habit. If you have been ill for some time you associate many places and situations with dread and seeing those situations may spark those memories and feelings. This is perfectly normal and means nothing.

Do not put added pressure on yourself by thinking about all the stages of the hierarchy you have yet to work through. That's bound to be discouraging because you can only envisage yourself tackling them in your present state of mind. Forget about all the stages except for the one you are working on. Try to regard the current stage as the only one you have to master.

When you come to tackle the situations higher up the hierarchy you will be in a better, improved state of mind. You will be more confident because of the successes you have achieved, you will be far more relaxed than now because of the lifestyle changes you've made and you will have improved your mastery of panic as a result of your experience in the phobic situations. The more you practise the easier it will become.

Early on you will be elated by every success. This is a wonderful spur. Unfortunately, it does not last. Soon you will find – incredible as it may seem – that each success is marked by nothing more than mild satisfaction. That in itself is a measure of how much progress you have made.

It makes your progress seem more substantial if you think of yourself not so much as someone working his way up through a hierarchy of situations but as someone learning to master panic. This means that every step in the hierarchy is as important as every other one.

At each stage you are learning to master your fear by accepting it, letting it wash over you. This means that an exercise in which you panic is not less useful or successful than one in which everything goes without a glitch. In this way you are able to appreciate that even apparent failures are an opportunity to build for success.

There is in fact no such a thing as failure. The only failure is not trying, not practising.

Celebrate your successes and admit it when you feel better. This is a way of making your progress real to you and it also helps those who care for you. It tells them that you are getting better. They too need encouragement. But warn them of the setbacks that will occur, explain to them that it is perfectly normal and perhaps ask them to remind you of this when they occur.

ESCAPE!

As you progress up through your hierarchy, preparing to tackle the next in vivo situation, you will be apprehensive about the prospect. This can be extremely disheartening.

At one stage I was practising every weekend on the Metrolink, Manchester's tram system. From Wednesday onwards, I started to become apprehensive. This apprehension was, at one stage, so unpleasant that I came to dread the end of the working week. Gradually and for no apparent reason, this apprehension began to diminish. I realised I had worked my way through it by continuing to practise.

It helps if you keep reminding yourself that this anticipatory fear is the worst part of the experience because it actually diminishes when you confront the real situation. Try to use this in a positive way. Keep reminding yourself that confronting the situation is easier than the anticipation.

Always be conscious of the fact that it is possible to slip back into old behaviour patterns. It will not happen provided you keep the new behaviour fresh through practice, and take care not to engage in those avoidance responses which fuel a phobic response.

In order to maintain your motivation it helps if you use what you know about positive reinforcement to confirm your progress. To help you do this you should work out ways in which you can reward yourself after every in vivo session. You can treat yourself to a cup of coffee and a cake in a café or buy a magazine. Buy yourself a meal, an article of clothing, a CD, book or whatever will reinforce your achievement. As soon as you complete the task you have set for yourself do something that gives you pleasure.

Above everything else it is the in vivo sessions that are the key to recovery. The rest of the programme is designed to make them possible and productive.

Once the time you have chosen to confront a phobic situation arrives, do not hesitate or make excuses to delay the actual practice or worse still, put it off till another day. Putting it off is always a mistake. You feel better today than you will tomorrow and by postponing the practice you are making the task more difficult for yourself. If you do it now you will have it over with whereas if you postpone it, it will seem a bigger ordeal.

No matter how well you prepare you will have to confront the moment when you enter the phobic situation. Always remember that it was avoidance behaviour that gave rise to your difficulties in the first place. This is the point at which you have to take a leap of faith and accept that nothing bad is going to happen to you.

ESCAPE!

Negative, frightening thoughts will start to emerge at this stage. Deal with them in the ways you have practised and go straight ahead with your session. Remember that there is no such thing as an unsuccessful exposure session.

Accept and deal with your unpleasant feelings and sensations. It is likely that you will feel worse in the early stages of the programme than at any other time. Feeling bad is not an indication that you are not making progress and certainly not a sign that things are getting worse.

If you feel anxious it is simply because you are beginning to confront your fear. By confronting them you will gradually reduce them. There is no doubt that the more you confront your fears and the more often you enter into the phobic situation, the more your anxiety symptoms will reduce until they are eventually under your control.

Remember at all times that you are not working according to a predetermined timetable. All that matters is that you continue to practise every week, as many times as you reasonably can. Aim for a minimum of two sessions a week. The more sessions you do and the longer their duration, the better your progress.

Do everything possible to make sure that nothing interrupts your weekly practise. You must give these sessions a high priority in your life. But do not put yourself under any time pressure to get through your hierarchies. Do not move on to the next stage in the ladder until you feel confident about the present one. Time spent mastering the early stages in the hierarchy is never wasted as it lays down solid foundations for total recovery.

Remember to attach proper significance to every piece of progress you make. Do not minimise or underestimate your achievements. Acknowledge them, celebrate them and mark them by giving yourself a reward. Relive it in your mind and savour the feelings of satisfaction and accomplishment. Do this immediately after the event, as soon as possible. This is an important part of your recovery.

You can speed your recovery if you remember that the longer the practice sessions, the more the progress. If you are practising travelling a single floor in a lift, for instance, the more often you repeat this during a session – travelling one floor and then getting out and doing it again – the better. This method is also more time effective.

Do not be discouraged if something you did with no difficulty last week provokes anxiety this week. This is no reflection on you. Nor is it a sign that something is wrong. Quite the contrary. This pattern of progress may be temporarily discouraging but it is perfectly normal.

Nor should you be concerned if, when you start confronting situations you've been avoiding for

ESCAPE!

some time you experience an outpouring of emotions you haven't felt recently. Perhaps this is because embarking on a programme of desensitisation is a life-enhancing decision and a turning point. It is common to start looking back over the sequence of events that brought you to this point. Do not be surprised if you feel a deep sense of regret or even anger at some of the things that have happened to you and some of the bad decisions you made in the past. You may well feel guilty about the ways your illness has impinged on the lives of others, particularly members of your family. This is perfectly normal and is nothing to worry about. Try to accept and express these feelings.

Keep right on to the end of the road. Recovery is likely to take at least six months and maybe as long as two years. From the outset you should be prepared to make this investment of time. Do not stop half way through thinking that you are happy with a partial recovery. Work right through to the end of your hierarchies. That is the only way to ensure that your progress is based on a secure foundation.

OVERCOMING SETBACKS

One thing is certain: you will have setbacks. How you react to them is entirely up to you. If you persist with your practice over the long run, the trend will be one of continued improvement and progress.

The greatest fear for anyone entering the phobic situation is that they will suffer an intolerable panic. This cannot happen. If you remember, phobics, looking back on their first panic attack, always exaggerate its intensity and discomfort. As with other things in life, so with panics: nothing ever matches the first one.

It is possible, however, though extremely unlikely, that the discomfort you experience in the phobic situation is more than you expected. Even after you have exhausted your armoury of coping strategies you may feel extremely tense. If this is so, do not worry. There are reasons for this.

It may be that you have not practised your relaxation techniques sufficiently. Before you can use them effectively in the phobic situation you must first master them under more favourable conditions in your home. You should be so familiar with the procedures for abdominal breathing, alternate nostril breathing, self-talk and all the other relaxation strategies that you can do them without thinking.

ESCAPE!

Another possibility is that you have not learnt to recognise the initial anxiety surge. Consequently you are not detecting and countering it as soon as it occurs. This delay allows anxiety to gather momentum and become more difficult to control.

It is also possible that you are not accepting your fear utterly, in the way discussed in Chapter 5. This is quite understandable. It is something you will master only with time and repeated practice. You must experience acceptance working on many occasions before it becomes automatic – just as the dysfunctional reaction that locked you into agoraphobia was once automatic.

The most likely explanation, however, is that you are tackling a situation too high up the hierarchy. You may object, saying that you have mastered the preceding step and this one, the one that is causing so much trouble, is the next one up.

May be so. But if it is giving you so much trouble, then it should not be the next one. Go back to your hierarchy and re-examine the task that is causing the problem and the one immediately before it. Are there any intermediate steps you can devise?

Let me give a concrete example. Step 3 in the bus hierarchy reads, 'I take the bus from town. I travel three stops on my own, without my helper, on a Saturday morning when the bus is fairly quiet.' This is causing problems. Step 2, which you have mastered is 'I take the bus from the end of the road. I travel three stops with my helper waiting for me at the third stop, on a Sunday morning when there are few passengers.'

You can create an intermediate step by having your helper wait at the third stop, reverting back to Sunday morning or taking the bus from the end of the road. Please do not regard such a change as a failure. You are simply ensuring that you are continuing to enter the phobic situation and therefore continuing your recovery. Simply put it down to experience.

After all, good days and bad days are the normal pattern of progress. A bad day is always disappointing – no matter how well prepared for it you are. Don't get it out of proportion. In the long term, it means nothing. It certainly does not mean that you are back to square one. It does not mean that you are not making progress.

What it means is that bad days are now so striking because they are no longer the norm. Do not lose heart and never think of using them as an excuse for giving up.

Whatever you do you must not try to justify giving up by claiming that you have tried really hard and still getting no better. May be you have tried – but if you do not seem to be getting better it is because you are failing to appreciate the improvements you are making. This is another reason why working through the hierarchy is so important – it lets you see how far you have come.

Beware of self-pity. When things are going badly, it's easy to fall into the "This is so unfair!" attitude. "Why should this happen to me? Why can't I be like everybody else?"

This self-indulgence is not helpful because we can so easily use it as an excuse for giving up. What's more, it's based on confused thinking.

Do you really believe that you are the only person in the world who has emotional problems? Do you think that you are the only agoraphobic? Of course not. Not only are you one among many, no matter how bad you feel there are certainly many hundreds of thousands of agoraphobics all over the world who are worse off than you. Many have not started to overcome their difficulties.

As you progress through the hierarchy you may find that your mood swinging between elation and despair. This is perfectly normal and harmless. Try to harness it to your advantage. Enjoy the elation – you've earned it. Appreciate how good it feels. But realise that it is not a permanent condition and that at some time it is likely to be replaced by despair. Tackle the despair in the same way you tackle all negative thoughts -- tell yourself that it is a normal part of the healing process and is a sign that you are getting better. It signifies nothing that should concern you.

MAINTAINING PROGRESS

You maintain progress by practising, by repeatedly confronting the phobic situations you avoided for so long.

By doing this you are drawing on the courage you have developed over many years and harnessing it to proven recovery techniques. Let nothing deflect you from your goal, which is total recovery.

All you will lose are your shackles. What you gain is a whole new life.

ESCAPE!

APPENDIX

TEST YOUR UNDERSTANDING (1) Answers

Answer yes or no to each of these questions. Check your answers in the Appendix.
6. No. Agoraphobia is not a sign of a nervous breakdown.
7. No. Agoraphobics generally have many other fears.
8. Yes. Agoraphobics commonly avoid public transport.
9. No. Some do but others fear going mad or making a fool of themselves when having a panic.
10. No. Avoidance reinforces fears.

Chapter 4: Challenging Damaging Thoughts

COGNITIVE DISTORTION SHEET

Negative thoughts: what exactly are you thinking?	Cognitive Distortion: What is wrong with this? (All-or-nothing, fortune-telling, emotional thinking etc?)	What evidence is there to disprove this distorted thinking?

Chapter 4. My Priorities. Using a separate box for each note down the five things that are most important to you. Consider relationships, family, work, hobbies, interests religious life and anything else that matters. Next to each jot down the number of hours you devote to it in the average week.

Things that are important to me. Jot down how much time you devote to each.	Ways in which I can develop these priorities.

Chapter 9 Constructing Hierarchies

Title of Hierarchy (e.g. buses, trains, trams.)

1. ....
2. ....
3. ....
4. ....
5. ....
6. ....
7. ....

ESCAPE!

8. ....
9. ....
10. ....
11. ....
12. ....
13. ....
14. ....
15. ....

Stresswatch

A non-profit making organisation established to help people with anxiety and phobic conditions. It provides training and free advice, details of which you will receive via a large stamped addressed envelope to Stresswatch, PO Box 4AR, London WIA 4AR.

Tranquilliser Withdrawal Support Group. You can get the details of your local group from MIND, The National Association for Mental Health, Granta House, 15-19, Broadway, Stratford, London E15 4 BQ.

Triumph Over Phobia (TOP U.K) Head Office, PO Box 1831, Bath BA1 3YX
Telephone: 01225 330353

The National Phobic Society, Zion Community Resource Centre, Hulme, Manchester. Telephone: 0161 881 1937

Joseph O'Neill

The Thanet Phobic Group. 47, Orchard Road, Westbrook, Margate, Kent. CT 9 5JS
Telephone: 0870 122 2325 www.phobics-society.org.uk

Bibliography

Withdrawing from tranquillisers and sleeping tablets: Coming off Tranquillisers and Sleeping Pills by Shirley Trickett.

YOGA

One of the best-selling writers on yoga is the American Richard Hittleman. This is because his books are extremely easy to follow and confined to the basics. They make an excellent starting point for anyone trying to learn the basics. Try his Yoga|: 28-Day Exercise Plan. Similarly,

The American Yoga Association's Easy Does It Yoga by Alice Christiansen is an excellent introduction.

Yoga: the Spirit & Practice of Moving into Stillness by Erich Schiffman;

ESCAPE!

MEDITATION

Chapter 6 contains all the information you need to get started with meditation. If, however, you would like to develop your interest further, that's fine but this is never a substitute for actually meditating. The best introduction is Meditation for Dummies by Stephen Bodian

FOR THE LOVE OF GOD

A good general book Bruce McClellan's Waters of Life: A Guide to Spiritual Reading provides and excellent overview of the available books.

There are many uplifting spiritual writers. Among the easiest to get to grips with are Anthony de Mello and Sister Wendy Beckett.

Gerald W Hughes is one of the leading writers on Christian prayer. His book, God of Surprises is a classic and essential for anyone interested in developing a prayer life.

CPSIA information can be obtained at www.ICGtesting.com
Printed in the USA
LVOW051957300513

336147LV00001B/9/P